English Learners / Students Acq

Test Preparat

McDougal Littell

McDougal Littell
A HOUGHTON MIFFLIN COMPANY
Evanston, Illinois • Boston • Dallas

ISBN 0-618-15827-8

4 5 6 7 8 9 CKI 04 03

Contents

Sección de Lectura: ¿Cuál es la pregunta y cómo la contesto?

WRITING SECTION:
What's the question and how do I answer it?

Sentence Completion

Writing Section

What's the question?

Some questions ask you to choose a grammatically correct word or phrase to complete a sentence. The directions read like this:

> **Read the passage and choose the word or group of words that belongs in each space. Mark the letter for your answer.**

The questions look like this:

You should be able to choose the right **verb tense and form**.	

Our vacation to California this summer was the best trip I have

ever __(1)__ . We went to the city my father lived in when he was a

boy, and it was the __(2)__ we had ever seen. My sister wanted to

stay at the playground, but I __(3)__ want to go. I wanted to go to

the beach. Eventually __(4)__ reached a compromise, and we went

to both places.

Labels:
- You should be able to choose the right **verb tense and form**.
- Here, you have to choose the right **form of an adjective**.
- You should also be ready to use **affirmatives** and **negatives** correctly.
- You are often asked to choose the correct **pronoun**.

1. **A** taken
   B took
   C been taking
   D had taken

2. **F** pleasant
   G most pleasant
   H more pleasant
   J most pleasantest

3. **A** did
   B didn't
   C not didn't
   D not gone

4. **F** she and I
   G she and me
   H me and her
   J her and I

TIP

Since many questions ask you to choose the correct verb tense or form, underline all the verbs and circle all the subjects as you read the paragraph.

Sentence Completion

Writing Section

How do I answer it?

Step 1: Read the passage. Underline all the main verbs in the paragraph. Circle all the subjects.

Step 2: Look at the answers for the first question. Read the sentence before and after the question.

Step 3: Cross out two answers you're pretty sure are wrong.

Step 4: To help you choose from the two remaining answers, here are a few tips:

- For **verb** questions, circle the subject of the sentence. Underline the verb in the sentence before and after it. Choose the answer that agrees with the subject and that is a matching tense.
- For **pronoun** questions, look at the sentence before and after. Circle the people or things that the pronoun is replacing.
- For **negative** questions, cross out answers that have double negatives.
- For **adjective** questions, look for clues like *than* (use a comparative, like nicer) or *the* before the blank (use the superlative, like *the best singer*).

Step 5: Choose your answer. Be sure you can give a reason that it's the best answer.

Step 6: Say the sentence silently with your answer choice in it. Say it two or three times.

Look at the model below. See how one student, Eric, went through steps 1–6 to answer a sentence completion question.

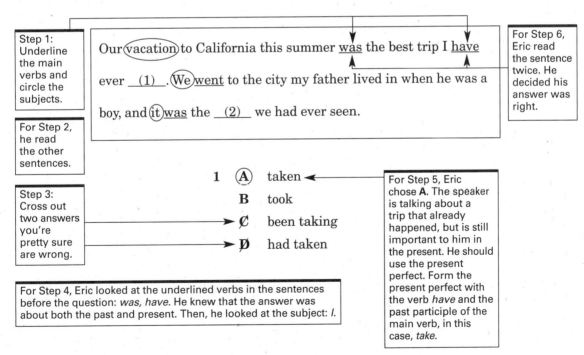

Sentence Completion

Writing Section

Practice Your Skills

ENGLISH

> **REMEMBER!**
> √ Underline all the verbs and circle all the subjects.
> √ Read the sentences before and after the question.
> √ Cross out two answers you're pretty sure are wrong.
>
> √ Look for clues in the sentence.
> √ Choose your answer and tell why.
> √ Say the sentence several times with your answer.

Now follow these steps to answer each of the questions below. Next to each question, write why your answer is right.

Read the passage and choose the word or group of words that belongs in each space. Mark the letter for your answer.

Some people complain that baseball is a game that __(1)__ move fast. Yet consider what the batter sees before the pitcher releases the ball. The pitcher __(2)__ on the mound, leaning toward home plate. __(3)__ watches the catcher give the sign for the pitch.

1 **A** doesn't
   B doesn't never
   C hardly doesn't
   D does not scarcely

   Why my answer is right:

   _____
   _____
   _____

2 **F** stands
   G stood
   H has stood
   J was standing

   Why my answer is right:

   _____
   _____
   _____

3 **A** I
   B It
   C They
   D He

   Why my answer is right:

   _____
   _____
   _____

Error Identification

Writing Section

What's the question?

There are questions that will ask you to identify errors or tell what is wrong in a sentence.

These mistakes are usually errors in spelling, punctuation, or capitalization.

The directions in the test look like this:

> **Read the passage and decide which type of error, if any, appears in each underlined section. Mark the letter for your answer.**

The questions look like this:

| You will be asked to find **Capitalization errors.** Capitalize names of specific places and persons, titles of works, and the first word of a sentence. | All ladies apparel is on sale now to celebrate the opening of our new store in <u>cisco</u>. ➤ **(1)** With every purchase of $50.00 or more, <u>customers will receive</u> **(2)** ◄ a <u>specal</u> scarf in blue or black. We are also giving away a free weekend <u>trip for two; so ask for</u> details when you come in. **(3)** ◄ <u>Act now</u>! ➤ **(4)** | You should be ready to spot **Spelling errors.** |
| You should also know when there is **No error.** | | Here you should find a **Punctuation error.** |

1	**A**	Spelling error		**3**	**A**	Spelling error
	B	Capitalization error			**B**	Capitalization error
	C	Punctuation error			**C**	Punctuation error
	D	No error			**D**	No error
2	**F**	Spelling error		**4**	**F**	Spelling error
	G	Capitalization error			**G**	Capitalization error
	H	Punctuation error			**H**	Punctuation error
	J	No error			**J**	No error

> **TIP**
>
> Always ask these questions:
>
> - **Spelling:** Are the underlined words missing any letters?
> - **Capitalization:** Are proper nouns capitalized? Is the beginning of the sentence capitalized?
> - **Punctuation:** Do sentences have periods and question marks? Are there commas before before words like *and, but, or for, so,* and *yet?*Are there commas before all items on a list? Are there commas before appositives (phrases that describe someone), like "John, the baseball player, is there"?

ENGLISH

Error Identification

Writing Section

How do I answer it?

Step 1: Take a minute to look at the passage. There may be words you haven't seen before, like place names. Use the rest of the sentence (the context) to get the meaning.

Step 2: Read the underlined section in each sentence. Decide what part of speech each word is. Is it a noun, a verb, an adjective or an adverb?

Step 3: Cross out two answers that you're pretty sure are wrong.

Step 4: Here are some tips to help you choose from the two remaining answers:

- Look for **spelling errors.** The word may have a missing letter or an extra one.
- Look for **capitalization errors** in nouns. Circle the nouns in a phrase. Are they proper nouns or generic nouns?
- Look for **punctuation clues** in the underlined phrase. Circle the words before and after the period, comma or other punctuation mark. Does the punctuation break the sentence where it's supposed to?
- Remember, only a few of the questions in the test are No error choices, so look very carefully before you choose this answer.

Step 5: Choose the best answer and tell why.

Look at the model below. See how one student, Elena, went through steps 1–5 to answer an error identification question.

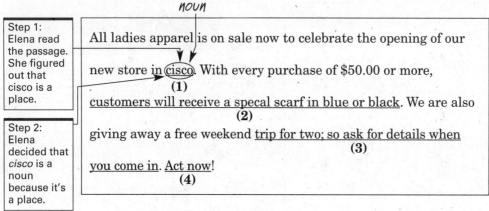

noun

Step 1: Elena read the passage. She figured out that cisco is a place.

All ladies apparel is on sale now to celebrate the opening of our

new store in (cisco). With every purchase of $50.00 or more,
(1)

customers will receive a specal scarf in blue or black. We are also
(2)

giving away a free weekend trip for two; so ask for details when
(3)

you come in. Act now!
(4)

Step 2: Elena decided that *cisco* is a noun because it's a place.

Step 3: Elena knew the period was correct, so she crossed out choices **C** and **D**.

1 A   Spelling error
   (B) Capitalization error
   C̸   Punctuation error
   D̸   No error

Step 5: Elena chose **B**. She proved her choice by saying that *cisco* is probably a town, and the names of towns have to be capitalized.

For Step 4, Elena thought that *cisco* was the name of a town—a proper noun. She wasn't sure about the spelling, but she knew it should begin with a capital letter.

Error Identification

Writing Section

Practice Your Skills

REMEMBER

√ Read the whole passage to look for context clues for words you may not understand.

√ Decide if each underlined word is a noun, verb, adjective, or adverb.

√ Cross out answers that you are pretty sure are wrong.

√ Look for words that give you clues about the right punctuation.

√ Look at nouns to find capitalization errors.

√ Look at words carefully to see if they have extra or missing letters.

√ Choose your answer and tell why.

Movies and television <u>can't compete, with</u> the reader's ability to fly away to King's Arthur's

                        (1)

court, explore the dingy streets of Charles Dicken's London, or laugh with Amy Tan when

she <u>revisites the crazy</u> world of her mother in *The Joy Luck Club*. Reading also keeps us

    (2)

abreast of the world around us, from Sammy Sosa's latest homerun to the best new <u>Night</u>

                                                      (3)

<u>Club</u> in town. <u>In addition, of course</u>, books can be read again and again.

         (4)

---

1 **A** Spelling error

    B Capitalization error

    C Punctuation error

    D No error

Why my answer is right:

_____

_____

_____

2 **F** Spelling error

    G Capitalization error

    H Punctuation error

    J No error

Why my answer is right:

_____

_____

_____

3 **A** Spelling error

    B Capitalization error

    C Punctuation error

    D No error

Why my answer is right:

_____

_____

_____

4 **F** Spelling error

    G Capitalization error

    H Punctuation error

    J No error

Why my answer is right:

_____

_____

_____

Revision in Context
Writing Section

What's the question?

There are questions that will ask you to find mistakes in the underlined sections of a passage. You then have to choose the right way to rewrite the sentence.

The questions ask you to figure out how sentences should be put together.

The directions in the test look like this:

> **Read the passage. Some sections are underlined. The underlined sections may be one of the following:**
>
> - **Incomplete sentences**
> - **Run-on sentences**
> - **Correctly written sentences that should be combined**
> - **Correctly written sentences that do not need to be rewritten**
>
> **Choose the best way to write each underlined section and mark the letter for your answer. If the underlined section needs no change, mark the choice "Correct as is."**

The questions look like this:

You will be asked to find **two correct sentences that need to be combined** (joined together).	Justin was excited when the Explorer's Club received permission to explore a remote cave. <u>It was virtually untouched</u> ►**(1)** <u>by modern man. That's why he looked forward to seeing the cave</u>. Justin was thrilled by the possibility of discovering ancient cave drawings.

<u>Justin was disappointed after exploring the cave, they had</u> **(2)** ◄ <u>found no drawings</u>. Just as the group was about to leave, his flashlight illuminated some letters carved into the wall. The letters read: "Wilkins 1886." <u>Those letters could have been carved by Clyde</u> **(3)** ◄ <u>Wilkins. The area's most notorious outlaw, who had evaded capture for years</u>. Could this cave have been his hideout?

You should be ready to spot **run-on sentences**.

Here you should find **incomplete sentences**.

> **TIP**
>
> Circle fragments *before* you read the answers.

Revision in Context

Writing Section

How do I answer it?

Step 1: Read the passage. Look for a subject and a verb in each underlined phrase. Circle the subject and the verb of the phrase.

Step 2: Decide what the problem is. Is it an incomplete sentence? Is it a run-on sentence, or do you see two sentences that need to be combined? Is it correct as is? Look for these problems:

	Problem	Example	How to fix it	Solution
Fragment	The sentence is missing a subject or a verb.	The area's most notorious outlaw, who had evaded capture for years.	• Add a subject and/or a verb • Combine the fragment with another sentence	<u>Those letters could have been carved by Clyde Wilkins</u>, the area's most notorious outlaw, who had evaded capture for years.
Two Short Sentences	Two short sentences need to be combined.	It was virtually untouched by modern man. That is why he looked forward to seeing the cave.	• Combine using **and, but, or, because** • Combine using **that, who, which**	He looked forward to seeing this cave <u>because</u> it was virtually untouched by modern man.
Run-on Sentence	One sentence has two different thoughts or actions.	Justin was disappointed after exploring the cave, they had found no drawings.	• Add a comma and **and, but,** or **or** • Combine using **because, since,** etc.	Justin was disappointed after exploring the cave <u>because</u> they had found no drawings.

Step 3: Before you read the answers, decide how you would correct the sentence. Say your answer twice.

Step 4: Cross out two answers that are definitely wrong.

Step 5: Choose the best answer and tell why.

Step 6: Read your answer. Underline the subject and verb, and make sure it is about a complete thought or action.

> **TIP**
> A run-on sentence often contains two sentences that express different thoughts or actions. Practice correcting run-ons using a comma and *and, but,* or *or:*
> Run-on: I was late for soccer practice, no one noticed.
> Correct: I was late for soccer practice, *but* no one noticed.

Revision in Context

Writing Section

Look at the model below. See how one student, Yukio, went through steps 1–6 to answer a Revision in Context question.

Step 1: Yukio circled the subject and a verb in each underlined phrase.

Justin was excited when the Explorer's Club received permission to explore a remote cave. (It was) virtually untouched by modern man. (That's) why he looked forward to seeing the cave.

(1)

Justin was thrilled by the possibility of discovering ancient cave drawings.

Step 2: Yukio decided that these were two sentences that needed to be combined.

Step 3: She thought about how she would combine the sentences: "Justin wanted to see the cave because it was untouched by modern man."

Step 5: Yukio looked at choices **B** and **D**. She knew choice **D** was wrong because modern man doesn't live in the cave. She decided **B** was the right answer.

Step 6: Yukio underlined the subject and verb: "He looked forward to seeing this cave because it was virtually untouched by modern man." She said the sentence in her own words: The cave was untouched, so Justin wanted to see it.

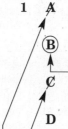

1   A It was virtually untouched by modern man since he looked forward to seeing this cave.

B He looked forward to seeing this cave because it was virtually untouched by modern man.

C It was virtually untouched by modern man, who looked forward to seeing this cave.

D He looked forward to seeing this modern man's cave that was virtually untouched.

Step 4: Yukio crossed out answers that were obviously wrong.

TIP

- Try combining the sentences in your own words *before* you read the answers.
- Don't worry if you don't understand every word in the paragraph. You can still choose the correct answer, for example, even if you don't know exactly what *virtually* means.

Revision in Context

Writing Section

Practice Your Skills

REMEMBER

√ Read the passage. Circle the subject and verb in each underlined phrase.

√ Decide what kind of error it is: an incomplete sentence, a run-on sentence, two sentences that need to be combined or correct as is.

√ Decide how you would correct the sentence before reading the answers.

√ Cross out the answers that are wrong.

√ Choose the best answer and tell why.

√ Read your answer. Underline the subject and verb. Tell the sentence's complete thought or action in your own words.

Now follow these steps to answer each of the following questions. Next to each question, write why your answer is right.

The Academy Awards will be presented on March 23 in Los Angeles. The celebrities are
(1)

growing excited. Famous people are getting ready for the big night. Especially the
(2)

women. The fashion industry is also excited. Many of the top designers offer to make

elaborate gowns for the stars attending the program there is so much interest in the
(3)

event. The media are stirred into action. Photographers arrive early. They come from all
(4)

over the world. Everywhere people watch and read about the big event. To see who is
(5)

wearing the most beautiful or most outrageous outfits.

---

1 A   The Academy Awards, will be presented,
       on March 23 in Los Angeles.

  B   The Academy Awards will be presented,
       on March 23 in Los Angeles.

  C   The Academy Awards will be presented,
       on March 23, in Los Angeles.

  D   Correct as is

Revision in Context

2 F Famous people are getting ready for the big night especially the women.

G Famous people, especially the women, are getting ready for the big night.

H Famous people are getting ready for the big night; especially the women.

J Correct as is

3 A Many of the top designers offer to make elaborate gowns for the stars attending the program; because there is so much interest in the event.

B Many of the top designers offer to make elaborate gowns for the stars attending the program. Because there is so much interest in the event.

C Many of the top designers offer to make elaborate gowns for the stars attending the program, because there is so much interest in the event.

D Correct as is

4 F Photographers arrive early, they come from all over the world.

G Photographers arriving early, they come from all over the world.

H Photographers from all over the world arrive early.

J Correct as is

5 A Most of them watch to see who is wearing the most beautiful or outrageous outfits.

B Most of them watch, to see who is wearing the most beautiful or outrageous outfits.

C Most of them watching to see who is wearing the most beautiful or outrageous outfits.

D Correct as is

Analogies

Writing Section

What's the question?

Some questions will ask you to make **analogies.** An analogy is a comparison of two pairs of words.

It compares how two things relate to each other. These things might not be similar.

Analogies are written like this:

giraffe: mammal :: grasshopper: insect

To read this analogy, you'd say, "*Giraffe* is to *mammal* what *grasshopper* is to *insect.*" That is, a giraffe is a type of mammal, just like a grasshopper is a type of insect.

The directions in the test look like this:

Each question below consists of a related pair of words or phrases labeled A through E. Select the pair that best expresses the relationship similar to that expressed in the original pair.

The questions look like this:

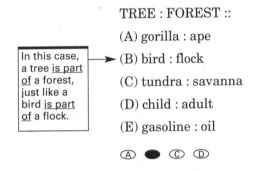

TREE : FOREST ::

(A) gorilla : ape

In this case, a tree <u>is part of</u> a forest, just like a bird <u>is part of</u> a flock.

(B) bird : flock

(C) tundra : savanna

(D) child : adult

(E) gasoline : oil

You might review the most common types of relationships used in analogies:

VIRUS: DISEASE :: carelessness : error	A *virus* <u>causes</u> *disease*, just like *carelessness* causes *error.*
FINGER: HAND :: chip : computer	A *finger* <u>is part of</u> a *hand*, just like a *chip* is part of a *computer.*
COLD : HOT :: arctic : tropical	*Cold* <u>is the opposite of</u> *hot*, just like *arctic* is the opposite of *tropical.*
CAR : TRANSPORTATION :: phone : communication	A *car* <u>is used for</u> *transportation,* just like a *phone* is used for *communication.*
COMPOSER : SYMPHONY :: architect : building	A *composer* <u>makes</u> a *symphony,* just like an *architect* makes a *building.*
OWL : NOCTURNAL :: lion : fierce	An *owl* <u>is usually</u> *nocturnal,* just like a *lion* is usually *fierce.*
ADD : INCREASE :: squander : decrease	To *add* <u>means the same as</u> to *increase.* To *squander* means the same as to *decrease.*
GO : WENT :: lose : lost	*Go* <u>is the present-tense form of</u> *went,* just like *lose* <u>is the present-tense form of</u> *lost.*

Analogies

How do I answer it?

Step 1: Figure out the relationship between the two words. Say the analogy as a sentence: "A tree <u>is part of</u> a forest."

Step 2: Look at the answer choices. Read each pair of words using the same phrase you used with the first two words: "A gorilla <u>is part of</u> an ape" (wrong).

Step 3: Cross out the choices that didn't make sense.

Step 4: Say the analogy as a full sentence. "A *Tree* <u>is part of</u> a *forest* just like a *bird* <u>is part of</u> a *flock*." Choose your answer.

Step 5: If there are two answers you think might be right, try choosing a different phrase. For example, "<u>There are a lot of</u> trees in the forest, just like <u>there are a lot of</u> birds in a flock." Then make your final choice.

Step 6: Read your choice again. Put the words for the answer choice first in the sentence: "A bird <u>is part of</u> a flock, just like a tree is part of a forest."

Look at the model below. See how one student, Mario, went through steps 1–6 to answer an analogy:

For Step 1, Mario read the two words given. He said it as a sentence. "A bailiff works in a court."

Step 3: He crossed out **C, D,** and **E.**

10 COURT : BAILIFF::

(A) school : janitor
(B) ranch : foreman ◄
(C̸) song : singer
(D̸) senator : congressman
(E̸) casino : gambler

For Step 5, Mario came up with a new phrase: <u>is in charge of</u>. He read both **A** and **B** in his new sentence:

A̸ A bailiff <u>is in charge of</u> a court, just like a janitor is in charge of a school.

B̸ A bailiff <u>is in charge of</u> a court, just like a foreman <u>is in charge of</u> a ranch.

Step 4: Mario was left with choices **A** and **B**. He said the analogy and chose **B**.

Step 6: Mario decided that B was the right answer. He read his choice again, putting the answer choice first : "*Ranch* is to *foreman* what *court* is to *bailiff*"

For Step 2, Mario looked at the answer choices. He read each one with the same phrase he used to read the first two words.

A   A bailiff <u>works in a</u> court, just like a janitor works at a school.

B   A bailiff <u>works in a</u> court, just like a foreman works at a ranch.

C̸   A bailiff <u>works in a</u> court, just like a singer works at a song.

D̸   A bailiff <u>works in a</u> court, just like a congressman works at a senator

E̸   A bailiff <u>works in a</u> court, just like a gambler works at a casino.

Analogies

Writing Section

Practice Your Skills

REMEMBER

√ Look at the two words given. Say the analogy as a sentence.

√ Read each answer using the same phrase you used with the first two words.

√ Cross out the choices that don't make sense.

√ Choose your answer. Say it as a sentence.

√ If there are two answers you think might be right, choose a different phrase. Then make your final choice.

√ Read your choice again.

TIP

If you don't know the meaning of a word, don't panic. Think of words that have similar or opposite meaning of the word that you do know. If it helps, draw a quick word web of the word you know. It may help you find out the meaning of the term you can't recognize.

Now follow the steps to answer each of the questions below. Next to each question, write why your answer is right.

Each question below consists of a related pair of words or phrases labeled A through E. Select the pair that best expresses the relationship similar to that expressed in the original pair.

1 ALMANAC : INFORMATION ::

(A) plant : flower
(B) notebook : paper
(C) woods : bear
(D) directory : names
(E) energy : fuel

Why my answer is right:

_____
_____
_____
_____
_____

2 PUZZLE : ENIGMATIC ::

(A) flower : aromatic
(B) plan : schematic
(C) satire : requisite
(D) intuition : rational
(E) sugar : candy

Why my answer is right:

_____
_____
_____
_____
_____

3 MUSIC : NOTES ::

(A) basket : reeds
(B) bucket : well
(C) camera : film
(D) car : road
(E) pen : ink

Why my answer is right:

_____
_____
_____
_____
_____

4 DILEMMA : RESOLUTION ::

(A) dialogue : discussion
(B) evidence : proof
(C) eyeglasses :
(D) skepticism : doubt
(E) disease : cure

Why my answer is right:

_____
_____
_____
_____
_____

Synonyms and Antonyms

Writing Section

What's the question?

There are questions that will ask you to choose the **synonym** or the **antonym** of a word.

A **synonym** has a meaning that's similar.
An **antonym** is a word that means the **opposite**.

Synonym Test

For the **synonym** test, the directions look like this:

Decide which word or phrase is most nearly the same in meaning as the word in capital letters. Fill in the circle containing the letter of your answer.

The questions look like this:

1 EXACT:
   (A) precise
   (B) narrow
   (C) clean
   (D) elderly
   (E) feminine

You will be asked to choose a word that means the **same** thing as EXACT. EXACT is the question word.

Antonym Test

For the antonym test, the directions look like this:

Decide which word is most nearly the opposite in meaning as the word in capital letters. Fill in the circle containing the letter of your answer.

The questions look like this:

1 TIDY:
   (A) limit
   (B) lost
   (C) square
   (D) messy
   (E) neat

You will be asked to find a word that means the **opposite** of TIDY. TIDY is the question word.

> **TIP**
> If the question word does not look familiar, don't be nervous. Give yourself time. You probably know more than you think.

Synonyms and Antonyms

Writing Section

How do I answer it?

Step 1: Read the directions carefully. Circle the word **same** or **opposite** in the directions.

Step 2: Underline parts of the word that you know. You may not know the word, but you might recognize a part of it. In a word like *unheard,* for example, you can underline the verb *heard.*

Step 3: Think of similar words. *Unheard* is like *unlikely, unhappy,* and *unbalanced.* See a pattern? These words mean not likely, happy, or balanced. If you think that *unheard* means *not heard,* you are right.

Step 4: Think of a sentence where you use the word. Sometimes the word is used in a common phrase, like *"That's unheard of!"*

Step 5: Decide if the word is positive or negative. Words beginning with *in-, un-,* and *dis-* turn a word into its opposite.

Step 6: Cross out answers that you're pretty sure are wrong. Choose the best answer and tell why. Try using your answer in the phrase from step 4 or in a new sentence.

> ## TIP
> In a **Synonym Test,** a word that has a different meaning from the question word is a wrong answer.
>
> In an **Antonym Test,** a word that has the same meaning as the question word is the wrong answer.

See how one student, Hassan, answered a synonym question:

Decide which word or phrase is most nearly the  same in meaning as the word in capital letters. Fill in the circle containing the letter of your answer.

Step 1: Hassan circled the word **same** in the directions.

Step 2: Hassan underlined *dis.* He'd seen it in words before.

1 DISREGARD:

→(A) consider
(B) ignore
→(C) look
→(D) obtain
→(E) read

Step 6: He thought that to *consider, read, look* and *obtain* were all positive things, so he crossed them out. He tried his answer in the phrase he remembered in Step 4: *ignore the law.* It made sense, so he chose **B**.

Step 3: Hassan remembered that **to diss someone** means to do something bad to him or her.

Step 4: Hassan remembered a phrase from TV: *disregard for the law.* It was about people who did not obey the law.

Step 5: Hassan was pretty sure the word is negative.

Synonyms and Antonyms

Writing Section

Practice Your Skills

REMEMBER!

√ Circle the word **same** or **opposite**.
√ Underline parts of the word that you know.
√ Think of words like it.
√ Think of how you've heard the word used.

√ Decide if the word is positive or negative.
√ Cross out wrong answers. Choose the best
answer and use it in a phrase or sentence.

Now follow these steps to answer each of the questions below.

Decide which word or phrase is most nearly the same in meaning as the word in capital letters. Fill in the circle containing the letter of your answer.

1 HYPOTHESIS: Ⓐ Ⓑ Ⓒ Ⓓ Ⓔ

    (A) side of a triangle
    (B) theory
    (C) needle
    (D) disease
    (E) report

2 VISAGE: Ⓐ Ⓑ Ⓒ Ⓓ Ⓔ

    (A) foreshadowing
    (B) face
    (C) outlook
    (D) eyesight
    (E) meeting

3 INFATUATED: Ⓐ Ⓑ Ⓒ Ⓓ Ⓔ

    (A) enamored
    (B) overweight
    (C) hinted at
    (D) meaningless
    (E) excited

Decide which word is most nearly the opposite in meaning as the word in capital letters. Fill in the circle containing the letter of your answer.

4 PROPRIETY: Ⓐ Ⓑ Ⓒ Ⓓ Ⓔ

    (A) alive
    (B) rudeness
    (C) ownership
    (D) purchase
    (E) hastiness

5 DISCORD: Ⓐ Ⓑ Ⓒ Ⓓ Ⓔ

    (A) music
    (B) creativity
    (C) doubt
    (D) emptiness
    (E) harmony

READING SECTION:
What's in the passage?

Hispanic Immigration in the 1960s

Reading Section

During the 1960s, the Hispanic population in the United States grew from 3 million to more than 9 million. This increased population came from a number of sources. Spanish-speaking Americans and Hispanics have always been a large and diverse group. America's Hispanic population includes people from many different areas such as Mexico, Puerto Rico, Cuba, the Dominican Republic, Central America, and South America. Because these groups all trace their roots back to Spanish-speaking countries, people often group them together. However, each group has its own history, its own pattern of settlement in the United States, and its own set of economic, social, cultural, and political concerns.

During the 1960s, the number of Mexicans settling in the United States rose. Mexican Americans, who have always been the largest Hispanic group in the United States, once lived mostly in the Southwest and California. Some were the children and grandchildren of the million or so Mexicans who settled in the United States in the decade following Mexico's 1910 revolution. Others came as *braceros,* or seasonal laborers, during the 1940s and 1950s.

Also in the 1960s about a million Puerto Ricans were identified as living in the United States. Most settled in the Northeast, with about 600,000 in New York City alone.

Facing discrimination and lacking needed skills and education, many Puerto Ricans had trouble finding work and getting ahead.

Hundreds of thousands of Cubans fled to the United States after the revolutionary leader Fidel Castro took over in 1959. Most settled in or near Miami, turning it into a boom town. Large Cuban communities also formed in New York City and New Jersey. Many Cubans were academics and professionals, such as doctors and lawyers, who fled to the United States to escape Castro's communist rule.

In addition, tens of thousands of Salvadorans, Guatemalans, Nicaraguans, and Colombians immigrated to the United States after the 1960s to escape civil war and chronic poverty.

Wherever they settled, during the 1960s many Hispanics found ethnic prejudice and discrimination in jobs and housing. Most lived in segregated *barrios,* or Hispanic neighborhoods. The Hispanic jobless rate was higher than that of whites. Many Hispanic families lived in poverty, in contrast to the relative wealth of the rest of the population.

It was time for Hispanics to act. They mobilized to action during the 1960s, 70s, 80s, and 90s, under such dedicated leaders as César Chávez and Dolores Heurta.

Percentage of Hispanic Population in the United States and Selected Metropolitan Areas, 1970–1994

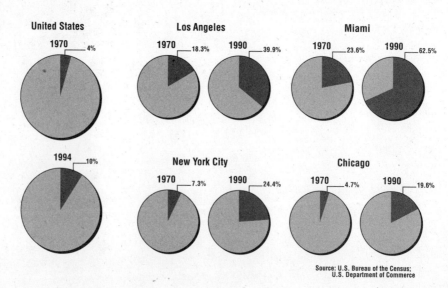

Source: U.S. Bureau of the Census;
U.S. Department of Commerce

Using Context Clues

Reading Section

What's in the passage?

Sometimes you won't understand every word in a reading passage. One thing you can do to figure out new words is to use **context clues.**

The **context** is the words, sentences, and ideas that come before and after a word or phrase.

When you read a passage, circle any new words that you don't understand. Then, look in the context to find clues—words or phrases that hint at what the new word means. Look at the circled words below and the type of context clues that hint at their meaning:

Type of clue	What it means	Example
Synonyms	a word that means the same thing as the new word	"ethnic prejudice and discrimination"
Antonyms	a word that means the opposite of the new word	"live in poverty, in contrast to the relative wealth of the rest of the population"
Definition	restating the new word by telling what it means	"came as braceros, or seasonal laborers"
Description	telling more about the new word	"the revolutionary leader Fidel Castro took over in 1959. . . escaping Castro's communist rule."
Example	giving an example of the new word	"Many Cubans were academics and professionals, such as doctors and lawyers."

> **TIP**
> Remember, you don't have to understand every word in a reading! Circle only the new words that are key to understanding the passage.

Using Context Clues

Reading Section

What's in the Passage?

To use context clues, follow these steps:

Step 1: Circle the word or phrase you don't understand.

Step 2: Underline key phrases and ideas in the sentence. Look for words that give synonyms, antonyms, examples, etc.

Step 3: Give the main idea of the paragraph the new word is in.

Step 4: Say the sentence in your own words.

Step 5: Guess at what the new word means. Use what you underlined to prove your guess is right.

In order to understand the word *segregated* in "Hispanic Immigration in the 1960s," one student, Kazuyo, followed these steps:

Step 1: Circle the word you don't understand.	Wherever they settled, during the 1960s many Hispanics found ethnic prejudice and discrimination in jobs and housing. Most lived in segregated *barrios,* or Hispanic neighborhoods. The Hispanic jobless rate was higher than that of whites. Many Hispanic families lived in poverty, in contrast to the relative wealth of the rest of the population. It was time for Hispanics to act. They mobilized to action during the 1960s, 70s, 80s, and 90s, under such dedicated leaders as César Chávez and Dolores Huerta.	Step 4: He said that this sentence is about Hispanics living in different or separate neighborhoods.
Step 2: Underline key or important ideas in the sentence before and after.		Step 5: Kayzo guessed that *segregated* meant *different* or *separate.*
Step 3: Kayzo said that the paragraph is about Hispanics being poor.		

Practice Your Skills

A. The following words and phrases are from the passage "Hispanic Immigration in the 1960s." Circle them in the passage and follow Steps 1–5 above to guess what they mean. Write your guess in the blanks.

My guess:

1. diverse   _____

2. pattern of settlement   _____

3. lacking   _____

4. mobilized   _____

Using Background Knowledge

Reading Section

What's in the passage?

Some passages may be about something you don't know a lot about. But you always know something about the topic. You can use your background knowledge—that is, what you already know about something—to figure out what the passage is about.

Before you read

Before you read the passage, you need to get an idea of the topic, or what the passage is about. Follow these steps:

Step 1: Circle the title of the passage.

Step 2: Circle the titles of any charts or graphs.

Step 3: Write the topic in your own words.

Step 4: Write 3–4 things you already know about the topic.

See how one student, Lisa, went through these steps before she read the passage:

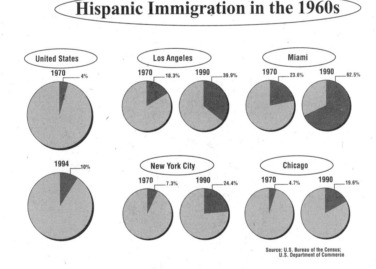

Hispanic Immigration in the 1960s

Step 1: Circle the title.

Step 2: Circle the titles of any charts or graphs.

Step 3: Lisa wrote what she thought the topic would be: Mexican people living in different cities in America.

Step 4: Lisa wrote four things she already knew about this topic:
1. A lot of Mexicans come to America.
2. A lot of Mexicans live in California because it's close to Mexico.
3. People from Cuba move to Miami a lot.
4. The news has stories about people in Miami being poor.

United States — 1970 — 4%
1994 — 10%

Los Angeles — 1970 — 18.3% — 1990 — 39.9%

Miami — 1970 — 23.6% — 1990 — 62.5%

New York City — 1970 — 7.3% — 1990 — 24.4%

Chicago — 1970 — 4.7% — 1990 — 19.6%

Source: U.S. Bureau of the Census; U.S. Department of Commerce

A. Look at the passage titles below. Write two things you already know about each one.

1. Up in Smoke: Cigarette Smoking

_____

2. Year-Round Schooling: A Good Idea

_____

3. Training Cats and Dogs

_____

Using Background Knowledge

Reading Section

What's in the passage?

As you read

As you read a passage, you will probably see new words you don't understand. You can use your background knowledge to figure out what they mean. Follow these steps:

Step 1: As you read, circle any new words you don't understand.

Step 2: Look at the words you circled. Figure out which ones are important and which ones you don't really need to know.

Step 3: Read the sentence before and after the new word. List two things you know about the topic.

Step 4: Guess at what the new word means. Give two reasons to support your guess.

See how Lisa followed steps 1–4 to figure out unfamiliar words in the passage, "Hispanic Immigration in the 1960s."

| Step 1: As Lisa read, she circled unfamiliar words. | Wherever they settled, during the 1960s many Hispanics found ethnic prejudice and discrimination in jobs and housing. Most lived in segregated barrios, or Hispanic neighborhoods. The Hispanic jobless rate was nearly 50 percent higher than that of whites. Many Hispanic families lived in poverty. | Step 4: Lisa figured out that ethnic had to do with being Hispanic. |

Step 2: Lisa didn't know what *segregated* meant, but she knew what a *barrio* was. She decided to figure out what *ethnic* meant.

Step 3: Lisa wrote two things she knew about discrimination and Hispanic neighborhoods:
1. Prejudice has to do with some people not liking Hispanics.
2. A lot of her Hispanic friends live in the barrios.

> **TIP**
> If you understand the main idea of a sentence without knowing the unfamiliar word, just skip it and keep reading.

A. The following words are from the passage "Hispanic Immigration in the 1960s." Use your background knowledge to figure out what they mean. Write what you already know in the blanks next to each word.

	My guess:	**What I Already Know about the Topic:**
1. segregated	_____	_____
2. revolutionary	_____	_____
3. trace their roots	_____	_____

READING SECTION:
What's the question and how do I answer it?

Writing by Moonlight

Murasaki Shikibu was an outstanding student, but her father was not proud of her. Instead, he wished she were a boy. In tenth-century Japan, girls were neither valued nor expected to excel in school.

However, Murasaki knew, for example, how to write and read in Chinese, even though many people thought women were not smart enough to learn such skills. Murasaki often had to hide her knowledge from others because she feared she would be rejected.

Despite her father's and society's disapproval, Murasaki was determined to be a writer. She liked to gaze at the moon and scribble by its light because no one bothered her at that time. People believed that women should not look at the moon because it allegedly caused them to age, and old women were not treated well. Murasaki did not care. She began referring to herself as a disgusting old fossil and kept staring at the moon. She was writing notes for a novel.

Fortunately, Murasaki's father found her a job as a lady-in-waiting, or servant, to the teenage empress. Murasaki had more time to write because the job was not demanding.

She disliked working at the palace, though, because people were occupied with gossip, bad poetry, and other shallow pursuits. Women and men were separated, and if a man entered a room, a woman had to go behind a screen. Everyone in the palace mocked Murasaki's work on her novel.

She continued to write, struggling with a lack of basic supplies such as ink and paper (the latter was rare in tenth-century Japan). The empress, who had heard that Murasaki knew Chinese, eventually solved that problem. She engaged Murasaki to teach her Chinese, even though society disapproved. In gratitude the empress gave Murasaki paper, ink, and brushes for writing.

Murasaki simplified her life so that she could devote most of her attention and energy to writing. She avoided social life in the palace, even during cold winters. She warmed her room by setting charcoal on fire in a hibachi. Her primary food was plain and dry rice cakes. Murasaki's only entertainment was playing gloomy music on a string instrument called a *koto*. Not surprisingly, she considered becoming a nun in the Buddhist faith.

Murasaki's devotion to writing paid off, although her accomplishments were not recognized for centuries. Many contemporary scholars believe that she wrote the first and oldest novel in human history—*The Tale of Genji*. Murasaki's novel revolutionized literature. She wrote about nature, people's feelings, and other topics in completely original ways. Some of her writing techniques were so advanced that they were not used again in literature for hundreds of years.

Ironically, despite her achievement, we do not know Murasaki's real name and never will. At that time, the names of Japanese women were not considered to be important. The name we know this author by today is a combination of her father's title and the name of the heroine of her famous novel.

Finding Supporting Evidence

Reading Section

What's the question?

Some questions ask you to choose an answer based on facts or evidence in the reading. The questions often look like this:

1   The passage provides evidence that
Murasaki is—

   A   determined

   B   lazy

   C   outgoing

   D   confused

First, be sure you understand the words in the question. These words may help:

provides evidence	*gives facts, clues*
sufficient	*enough*
suggests that	*hints that*
shows how	*proves*
reveals	*tells you how*

Such questions ask you to choose an answer that you can prove is true. You should only choose an answer if you can find evidence in the passage that proves it is true.

> **TIP**
> When you take the test, try saying the question like this:
> **The reading says that...**

A. Try rewriting each one of the following questions. The first one is done for you.

  1. The passage provides evidence that Murasaki is—

    The reading says that Murasaki is _____

  2. The writer suggests that Murasaki—

    _____

  3. The words show how Murasaki—

    _____

Finding Supporting Evidence

Reading Section

How do I answer it?

Step 1: Look at the answers. Cross out two you are pretty sure are wrong.

Step 2: Go back to the reading. Look for words or phrases in the answers.

Step 3: Underline phrases in the reading that prove one answer is right.

Step 4: Choose the answer you think is right.

Step 5: Read what you underlined in the reading again. Does it prove your answer choice?

> ### TIP
> Remember that evidence and clues may hint at a statement—not restate it exactly.

Look at the model below. See how one student, Sara, went through steps 1–5 to answer a question about the passage "Writing by Moonlight."

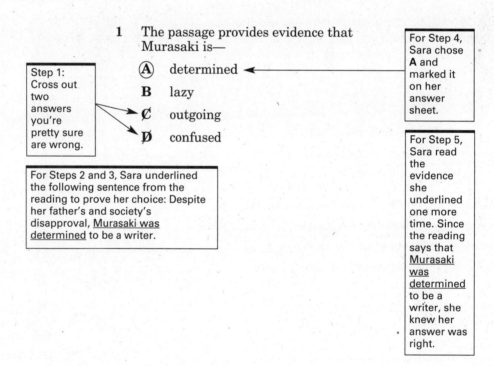

1   The passage provides evidence that Murasaki is—

  Ⓐ   determined

  B   lazy

  Ȼ   outgoing

  Ḏ   confused

Step 1: Cross out two answers you're pretty sure are wrong.

For Steps 2 and 3, Sara underlined the following sentence from the reading to prove her choice: Despite her father's and society's disapproval, <u>Murasaki was determined</u> to be a writer.

For Step 4, Sara chose **A** and marked it on her answer sheet.

For Step 5, Sara read the evidence she underlined one more time. Since the reading says that <u>Murasaki was determined</u> to be a writer, she knew her answer was right.

Finding Supporting Evidence

Reading Section

Practice Your Skills

> **REMEMBER!**
> √ Cross out two answers.
> √ Look for words from the answers in the reading.
> √ Underline supporting evidence in the reading.
> √ Choose your answer.
> √ Explain your answer.

The following questions refer to the passage "Writing by Moonlight." Read each one and choose your answer. Copy the evidence from the reading in the spaces next to each question.

1 The passage reveals that—

    A Murasaki disliked being a student

    B girls were not valued as students in tenth-century Japan

    C girls were not valued as servants in tenth-century Japan

    D the empress had many servants

Evidence

_____

_____

_____

_____

2 Murasaki shows that she does not enjoy the palace by—

    F writing notes for a novel

    G attending school

    H gazing at the moon

    J passing time in her room

Evidence

_____

_____

_____

_____

3 The passage provides sufficient evidence to show that Murasaki—

    A should not have learned Chinese

    B deserves recognition for her accomplishments

    C did not like living simply

    D should not have looked at the moon

Evidence

_____

_____

_____

_____

Determining Purpose

Reading Section

What's the question?

Some questions ask you to identify the main point of a passage. These questions ask you to **determine purpose.** The questions might look like this:

1. The author's main point is to—
2. The author's purpose in writing this passage is to—
3. The main purpose of the paragraph is to—
4. What is the point of this essay?

First, be sure you understand the words in the question. These words may help:

main point	*central idea, most important*
purpose	*intent, goal*
in order to	*so he/she can*

These questions are asking you to decide why the reading, or a part of the reading, was written. You should choose an answer that explains why the writer wrote the passage.

TIP

Be sure to mark the part of the passage the question asks about. Here are some clues:

initial, opening paragraph	*first paragraph*
final, closing paragraph	*last paragraph*

A. Circle the part of the reading each question asks about. Then circle the phrase that tells you this. Underline the words *purpose, reason,* or *main point* in the question. The first one is done for you.

	Paragraph
1. The author's <u>purpose</u> in writing the ⟨opening paragraph⟩—	①2 3 4 5 6 7 8 9 10
2. The main point of the second sentence of the closing paragraph is to—	1 2 3 4 5 6 7 8 9 10
3. This essay is saying that—	1 2 3 4 5 6 7 8 9 10
4. The main purpose of the final paragraph is to—	1 2 3 4 5 6 7 8 9 10
5. The author wrote the initial paragraph in order to—	1 2 3 4 5 6 7 8 9 10

Determining Purpose

Reading Section

How do I answer it?

Step 1: Read the question. Circle the part of the reading the question asks about. Underline words like *reason*, *purpose*, or *main point*.

Step 2: Look at the answers. Cross out two you are pretty sure are wrong.

Step 3: Go back to the circled section. Find who or what the central point is.

Step 4: Underline phrases that describe this central person or thing and/or how it acts.

Step 5: Read your answer choices carefully. Choose the most likely answer.

Step 6: Read what you underlined. Does it prove your answer choice?

Look at the model below. See how one student, Jamal, went through steps 1–6 to answer a question about part of "Writing by Moonlight."

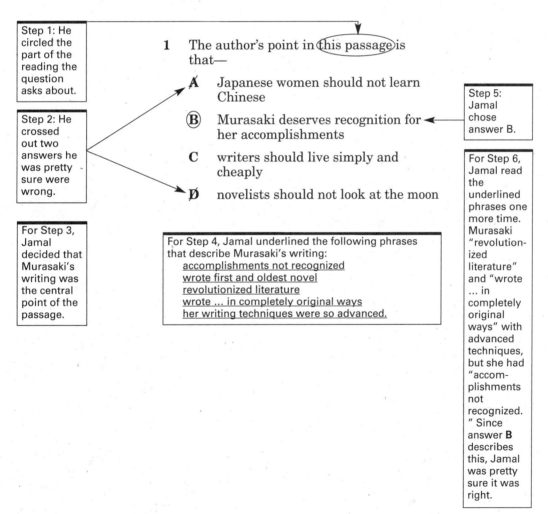

Step 1: He circled the part of the reading the question asks about.

Step 2: He crossed out two answers he was pretty sure were wrong.

For Step 3, Jamal decided that Murasaki's writing was the central point of the passage.

1 The author's point in this passage is that—

A Japanese women should not learn Chinese

B Murasaki deserves recognition for her accomplishments

C writers should live simply and cheaply

D novelists should not look at the moon

Step 5: Jamal chose answer B.

For Step 4, Jamal underlined the following phrases that describe Murasaki's writing:
accomplishments not recognized
wrote first and oldest novel
revolutionized literature
wrote ... in completely original ways
her writing techniques were so advanced.

For Step 6, Jamal read the underlined phrases one more time. Murasaki "revolutionized literature" and "wrote ... in completely original ways" with advanced techniques, but she had "accomplishments not recognized." Since answer B describes this, Jamal was pretty sure it was right.

Determining Purpose

Reading Section

Practice Your Skills

> **REMEMBER!**
>
> √ Underline words like *reason* and *purpose* in the question. Circle the part of the reading the question asks about.
>
> √ Cross out two answers you are pretty sure are wrong.
>
> √ Find the main point and underline phrases about it.
>
> √ Choose the most likely answer.
>
> √ Use what you underlined to prove your answer choice.

The following questions refer to the passage "Writing by Moonlight." Read each one and choose your answer. Copy what you underlined in the reading to prove your choice in the spaces next to each question.

1 The author wrote Paragraph 3 in order to—

   A show that Murasaki persisted in spite of much disapproval.

   B describe the beliefs of tenth-century Japan.

   C show how Murasaki was acting foolishly.

   D warn people about looking at the moon.

DESCRIPTIVE INFORMATION:

_____

_____

_____

_____

2 The purpose of describing Murasaki's life in Paragraph 7 is to—

   F describe typical palace life.

   G show that Murasaki was a poor servant.

   H show her dedication to writing through difficult conditions.

   J describe Murasaki's entertainment.

DESCRIPTIVE INFORMATION:

_____

_____

_____

_____

3 With this essay, the author is making the point that—

   A Murasaki did not like cold winters, gossip, or joyful music.

   B it is foolish to stare at the moon.

   C women were not treated well in tenth-century Japan.

   D despite opposition, Murasaki wrote what was probably the first novel.

DESCRIPTIVE INFORMATION:

_____

_____

_____

_____

The Aztecs Control Central Mexico   *Reading Section*

Aztecs Build an Empire

The Aztecs arrived in the Valley of Mexico around A.D. 1299. It was the home of several small cities that had survived the end of Toltec rule. The Aztecs, who were then called the Mexica, were a poor, nomadic people. Fierce and ambitious, the Aztecs soon adapted to local ways. They found paid work as soldiers for local rulers.

According to an Aztec legend, the Aztecs' sun god, Huitzilopochtli (wee-tsee-loh-POHCH-tlee), told them to start a city of their own. He said to look for a place where an eagle stood on a cactus, holding a snake in its mouth. Part of the legend is told with these words:

> The place where the eagle screams,
> where he spreads his wings;
> the place where he feeds,
> where the fish jump,
> where the serpents
> coil up and hiss!
> This shall be Mexico Tenochtitlán
> and many things shall happen!
> —Cronica Mexicayotl

The Aztecs found this place on a small island in Lake Texcoco, at the center of the valley. There, in 1324, they started their city and named it Tenochtitlán (the-NOCH-tee-TLAHN).

Aztecs Grow Stronger

In 1428, the Aztecs joined with two other cities—Texcoco and Tlacopán—to form the Triple Alliance. This group of cities became the leading power in the Valley of Mexico. The Triple Alliance soon gained control over neighboring regions. By the early 1500s, the alliance controlled the huge area that stretched from central Mexico to the Atlantic and Pacific coasts and south into Oaxaca. Their empire was divided into 38 provinces, or states. It had an estimated population of between 5 and 15 million people.

The Aztec state was powerful because of its military rule and its wealth from the taxes paid by the people it conquered. The Aztecs loosely controlled most of their empire. They often let local leaders rule their own regions. The Aztecs did demand tribute, however, of gold, corn, cocoa, cotton, jade and other products. If local rulers refused to pay tribute, the Aztec warriors responded brutally. They destroyed villages and captured or killed the people.

Problems in the Aztec Empire

Eventually, the Aztecs' huge empire caused problems for them. In 1502 a new ruler, Montezuma II, became emperor. Under Montezuma, the Aztec empire began to weaken. For nearly a century, the Aztecs had been demanding tribute and sacrifices from the provinces. Now, with the population of Tenochtitlán growing, the emperor demanded even more tribute and sacrifices. Some provinces revolted. The people were unhappy with the cruel and demanding Aztecs. These revolts were the beginning of a period of instability and unrest. During this time, the Aztec military was often sent to the provinces to stop rebellions.

Montezuma tried to reduce pressure on the provinces. He reduced the number of government officials. Still, the people in the provinces were unhappy and resentful. Then, in addition to the problems at home, another threat appeared: the arrival of the Spanish.

ENGLISH

Making Inferences

What's the question?

Some questions ask you to make inferences based on a reading. The questions might look like this:

1. From this passage, you can infer—
2. According to the author, one has reason to believe—
3. The second paragraph suggests that—
4. Based on the information, one can tell that—
5. Information in the passage suggests that—
6. What probably made the Azetecs good warriors was—

First, be sure you understand the words in the question. These words may help:

infer	*figure out, guess*
gives (one) reason to believe	*makes you think that*
suggest	*give clues about, hint*
(you) can tell that	*there is proof to show that*
probably	*most likely*

These questions are asking you to make a guess based on clues in the passage. You should choose an answer that you can figure out from phrases in the reading.

> **TIP**
> The exact answer isn't in the reading. Try to figure out the best answer based on two or three clues in the reading.

A. Underline the word or phrase that tells you to make an inference in each question below. Then circle what the question is asking about. The first one is done for you.

1. The fact that the Aztecs found paid work as soldiers suggests that—
2. The alliance with Texcoco and Tlacopán gives one reason to believe—
3. From Montezuma's actions you can tell that—
4. From the empire's wealth, you can infer that—
5. According to the author, one can tell that—

Making Inferences

Reading Section

How do I answer it?

Step 1: Underline words or phrases in the question that tell you to make an inference. Circle what the question is asking about.

Step 2: Read the answers carefully. Cross out two you are pretty sure are wrong.

Step 3: Go back to the reading. Underline phrases that tell about the subject or main point.

Step 4: Read your answer choices. Then read over the phrases that you underlined. Choose the answer most supported by information in the reading.

Step 5: Read what you underlined in the reading. Does it support your answer choice?

Look at the model below. See how Li went through steps 1–5 to answer a question about the passage "The Aztecs Control Central Mexico."

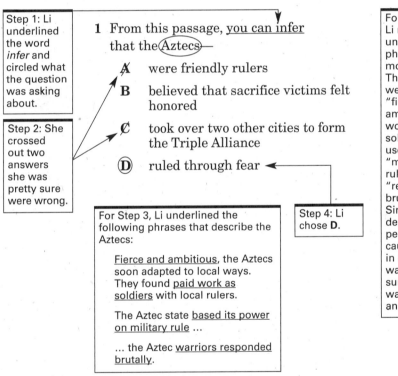

Step 1: Li underlined the word *infer* and circled what the question was asking about.

Step 2: She crossed out two answers she was pretty sure were wrong.

1 From this passage, <u>you can infer</u> that the (Aztecs)—

A̶ were friendly rulers

B believed that sacrifice victims felt honored

C̶ took over two other cities to form the Triple Alliance

(D) ruled through fear ◄

For Step 3, Li underlined the following phrases that describe the Aztecs:

<u>Fierce and ambitious</u>, the Aztecs soon adapted to local ways. They found <u>paid work as soldiers</u> with local rulers.

The Aztec state <u>based its power on military rule</u> ...

... the Aztec <u>warriors responded brutally</u>.

Step 4: Li chose **D**.

For Step 5, Li read the underlined phrases one more time. The Aztecs were "fierce and ambitious," worked "as soldiers," used "military rule," and "responded brutally." Since these describe a people that caused fear in others, Li was pretty sure that **D** was the answer.

ENGLISH

Making Inferences

How do I answer it?

> ### REMEMBER!
>
> √ Underline phrases like *suggest* and *you can tell* in the question. Circle the main point.
>
> √ Read the answers. Cross out two answers you're pretty sure are wrong.
>
> √ In the reading, underline phrases that give clues about the answer.
>
> √ Choose the answer you can figure out from two or three clues in the passage.
>
> √ Read your underlined clues again. Is your answer right?

The following questions refer to the passage "The Aztecs Control Central Mexico." Read each one and choose your answer. Write what the question is asking about and copy clues from the reading that supports your answers.

1   The fact that Aztecs worked as paid soldiers suggests that they—

   A   learned military skills before forming an empire

   B   needed to protect their way of life

   C   did not like their current home

   D   were ready to move to a new valley

Topic/Clues:

_____

_____

_____

_____

2   The alliance with Texcoco and Tlacopán gives one reason to believe—

   F   these two cities were weak

   G   the Aztecs were weaker than these two cities

   H   the Aztecs did not war with all their neighbors

   J   the Aztecs enjoyed life as nomads

Topic/Clues:

_____

_____

_____

3   From Montezuma's actions you can tell that—

   A   the Aztecs were becoming more religious

   B   the population enjoyed being part of a large empire

   C   he had weak control of his empire

   D   he did not want to be emperor

Topic/Clues:

_____

_____

_____

_____

Making Predictions

Reading Section

What's the question?

Some questions ask you to choose an answer based on what you think might happen next in the reading. These questions ask you to **make predictions.** The questions usually look like this:

1. The Aztecs' empire will most likely—

2. You can tell from the passage that the Spanish will probably—

3. What is Montezuma likely to do next?

4. Judging by the passage, which action will the Spaniards most likely take?

5. Which of the following is least likely to happen?

First, be sure you understand the words in the question. The phrases that follow may be used in questions that ask you to make predictions. Look at their meanings.

most likely   *will probably*
least likely   *will probably not*
you can tell   *you can figure out*

These questions are asking you to guess what someone will do or what might happen next. You should choose an answer based on what has already happened in the passage.

Read the question carefully. Follow these steps:

Step 1: Underline the main subject—that is, the person or thing that you're making a prediction about.

Step 2: If the question has a time period *(this evening, in the future, next),* circle it.

Step 3: If the question has the word *least* or *not* in it, underline that word twice.

Look at how one student, Maria, went over the question below:

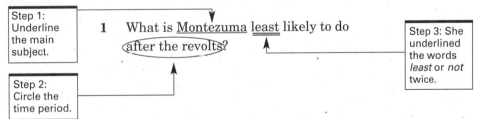

A. Read each of the following questions carefully. Underline the main subject. If there is a time frame, circle it. If the word *least* or *not* is in the question, underline that word twice.

1. In the future the Aztecs' empire will most likely—

2. You can tell from the passage that the Spanish will probably not—

3. What will Montezuma be least likely to do next?

4. Which of the following is likely to happen after the Spanish arrive?

Making Predictions

Reading Section

How do I answer it?

Step 1: Read the question. Underline the main subject. If there is a time period, circle it. If the word *least* or *not* is in the question, underline it twice.

Step 2: Look at the answers carefully. Cross out the two answers you are pretty sure are wrong.

Step 3: Go back to the reading. Underline clues about the feelings or actions of the subject.

Step 4: In the reading, underline what has already happened.

Step 5: Read your answer choices carefully. Choose the most likely answer. Make your choice based on what you underlined.

Step 6: Read your underlined clues again. Do they support your answer choice? Read your answer again.

Look at the model below. See how Maria went through steps 1–6 to answer a question about the passage "The Aztecs Control Central Mexico."

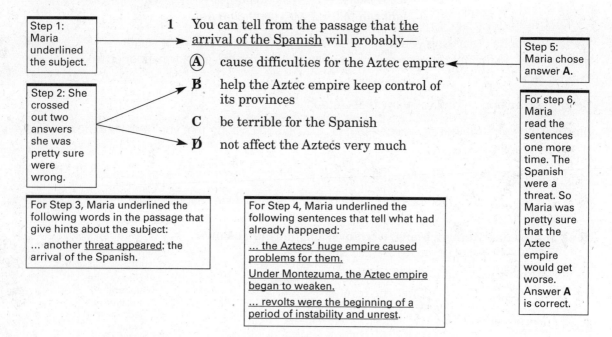

Step 1: Maria underlined the subject.

1 You can tell from the passage that <u>the arrival of the Spanish</u> will probably—

Ⓐ cause difficulties for the Aztec empire

Ⓑ help the Aztec empire keep control of its provinces

C be terrible for the Spanish

Ⓓ not affect the Aztecs very much

Step 5: Maria chose answer **A**.

Step 2: She crossed out two answers she was pretty sure were wrong.

For Step 3, Maria underlined the following words in the passage that give hints about the subject:

... another <u>threat appeared</u>; the arrival of the Spanish.

For Step 4, Maria underlined the following sentences that tell what had already happened:

... <u>the Aztecs' huge empire caused problems for them.</u>

<u>Under Montezuma, the Aztec empire began to weaken.</u>

... <u>revolts were the beginning of a period of instability and unrest.</u>

For step 6, Maria read the sentences one more time. The Spanish were a threat. So Maria was pretty sure that the Aztec empire would get worse. Answer **A** is correct.

> **TIP**
> When you cross out answers, cross out the letter only. After you go through all the steps, you might decide that one of these answers is right after all.

Making Predictions

Reading Section

Practice Your Skills

REMEMBER!

√ Read the question. Underline the subject. Circle the time frame. Underline the words *least* and *not* twice if they appear.

√ Cross out two answers you're pretty sure are wrong.

√ In the reading, underline clues about the subject.

√ Underline what has already happened.

√ Choose your answer.

√ Check your answer against what you found in the reading.

The following questions refer to the passage "The Aztecs Control Central Mexico." Read each one and choose your answer. Copy what you found in the reading to support your choice in the spaces next to each question.

CLUES:

1   The Spanish will probably not—

   A   help Montezuma with the empire

   B   conquer the Aztecs

   C   contribute to Montezuma's difficulties

   D   battle the Aztecs

_____

_____

_____

_____

CLUES:

2   What will Montezuma be least likely to do next?

   F   look for ways to stop revolts

   G   maintain the number of officials

   H   resist Spanish influence

   J   welcome the support of the Spanish

_____

_____

_____

_____

CLUES:

3   After the Spanish arrive, the Aztecs' empire will most likely—

   A   remain the same

   B   continue to do poorly

   C   increase its wealth

   D   celebrate

_____

_____

_____

_____

Built for Speed

According to some scientists, the enormous dinosaur *Tyrannosaurus rex* could run as fast as 34 miles per hour (mph). This huge creature could achieve such high speeds because it had unusually large thigh muscles.

However, a *Tyrannosaurus rex* could not move as quickly as a modern-day whippet (a type of dog), horse, or cheetah. All of those animals can run at speeds of more than 40 mph. Human beings, although they did not exist while dinosaurs were alive, would have been comparatively slow and easy prey for a *Tyrannosaurus rex*. A person's maximum speed is 23 mph.

Biped mammals, those that walk and run on two legs, include human beings. People cannot achieve the high speeds of quadrupeds—animals that walk and run on four legs—because two of their limbs, the arms, are hanging uselessly at their sides.

Horses are quadrupeds that can use all four limbs when running, which enables a maximum speed almost twice as fast as that of human beings. When horses run, they never have more than two hooves touching the ground. Horses have no ground contact at all for about a quarter of the time they run. This enables them to achieve a maximum speed of 43 mph.

Whippets and cheetahs stay off the ground even longer while they run—they are airborne for about twice the time that a cantering horse is. Cheetahs, the speediest mammals on the planet, have hip joints and shoulder blades that move easily. In addition, they have very flexible skeletons that allow their backbones to ripple up and down during a run. These features give cheetahs the ability to lengthen their stride—to about twice that of a horse—and move their legs very fast.

This ability to attain a high running speed is not as useful as it might seem. Humans and horses cannot run as fast as cheetahs, but they have good endurance. Cheetahs have such poor endurance that they can only keep up their maximum speed for about 15 seconds. Consequently, if a slow but determined *Tyrannosaurus rex* had encountered a modern-day cheetah, that dinosaur could have caught the fastest mammal on Earth.

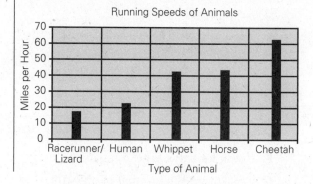

Running Speeds of Animals

Choosing the Main Idea

Reading Section

What's the question?

Some questions ask you to choose the main idea of the reading. The main idea is the key point of a paragraph or passage. The questions often look like this:

1. The passage evaluates—

2. Which statement best expresses the main idea in Paragraph 5?

3. According to the passage, speed—

4. The main idea of the final paragraph—

First, be sure you understand the words in the question. You should know these words and phrases:

evaluates	*compares, tells, judges*
expresses	*says, talks about*
according to	*because of what it says*

These questions are asking you to decide what the main idea of a passage is. You should choose an answer that tells about all the ideas in a passage.

Read the question carefully. Follow these steps:

Step 1: Underline the words *evaluate, express, according to,* or *main idea.*

Step 2: If the question has a subject, underline it twice.

Step 3: Within the question, circle the part of the reading the question is about.

See how one student, Winston, followed these steps:

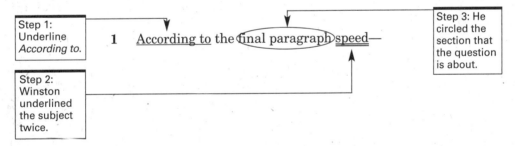

A. Read each of the following questions carefully. Underline words like *evaluate, express,* and *according to.* Underline the subject twice. Circle the section of the reading.

1. The first paragraph evaluates—

2. Which statement best expresses the main idea in Paragraph 5?

3. According to the third paragraph, biped mammals—

4. The main idea of the final paragraph—

Choosing the Main Idea

Reading Section

How do I answer it?

Step 1: Read the question. Underline the words *evaluate*, *express*, *according to*, or *main idea*. Underline the subject twice.

Step 2: Circle the section of the reading the question is about.

Step 3: Cross out the answers that aren't true and that are not mentioned in the reading.

Step 4: Read your answer choices carefully. Choose the answer you think is correct.

Step 5: Go back to the passage. Underline a sentence in each paragraph that supports your answer. If the passage is only one paragraph, underline the subject and verb of each sentence in it.

Step 6: Read over what you have underlined. Explain how it proves your choice.

Look at the model below. See how Winston went through steps 1–6 to answer a question about the passage "Built for Speed."

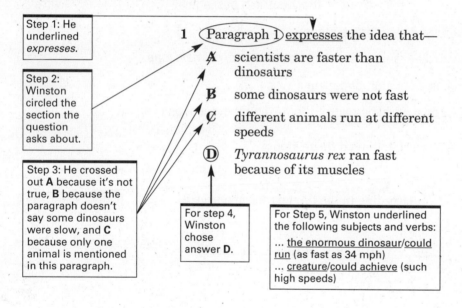

Step 1: He underlined *expresses*.

Step 2: Winston circled the section the question asks about.

Step 3: He crossed out **A** because it's not true, **B** because the paragraph doesn't say some dinosaurs were slow, and **C** because only one animal is mentioned in this paragraph.

1 Paragraph 1 expresses the idea that—

A   scientists are faster than dinosaurs

B   some dinosaurs were not fast

C   different animals run at different speeds

D   *Tyrannosaurus rex* ran fast because of its muscles

For step 4, Winston chose answer **D**.

For Step 5, Winston underlined the following subjects and verbs:
... the enormous dinosaur/could run (as fast as 34 mph)
... creature/could achieve (such high speeds)

For Step 6, Winston read what he underlined. He saw that each subject referred to *Tyrannosaurus rex*. Each verb led to a statement about speed. He knew **D** was the right answer.

Choosing the Main Idea

Practice Your Skills

> **REMEMBER!**
> √ Read the question. Underline the words *express*, *evaluate*, and *according to*. Underline the subject twice.
> √ Circle the part of the passage the question asks about.
> √ Cross out answers that are untrue or not mentioned in the section.
>
> √ Choose your answer.
> √ In the section, underline main sentences in each paragraph or the subject and verb in each sentence.
> √ Explain how what you underlined proves your choice is right.

The following questions refer to the passage "Built for Speed." Read each one and choose your answer. Copy what you found in the reading to support your choice in the spaces next to each question.

1   This main idea of the final paragraph is that—

A   some animals run faster than others

B   animals can be taught to run faster

C   human beings can sometimes run faster than whippets

D   endurance can sometimes be more important than speed

SUPPORTING INFORMATION:

_____

_____

_____

_____

2   According to the passage,—

F   dinosaurs had good hunting habits

G   human beings need to learn to run faster

H   different animals run at different speeds

J   speed is more important than endurance

SUPPORTING INFORMATION:

_____

_____

_____

_____

3   Paragraph 3 explains—

A   why people are faster than mammals with four legs

B   why people don't have four legs

C   why mammals with four legs are faster than mammals with two

D   why mammals with two legs have two useless limbs

SUPPORTING INFORMATION:

_____

_____

_____

_____

Choosing the Best Summary

Reading Section

What's the question?

Some questions ask you to choose an answer that gives a **summary** of what is in the reading. They often look like this:

> **1** Which of the following best summarizes Paragraph 2?
>
> **A** It would be easy for a human to escape a *Tyrannosaurus rex*.
>
> **B** A *Tyrannosaurus rex* would not be as fast as a whippet, horse, or cheetah, but would be faster than a human.
>
> **C** Whippets, horses and cheetahs are lucky that *Tyrannosaurus rex* does not live today.
>
> **D** It is unfortunate for *Tyrannosaurus rex* that it did not have humans for prey.

First, be sure you understand the words in the question. Any of the phrases below may be used when a question asks you to choose the best summary. They ask you to choose the best short version of a passage.

summarize	**give a synopsis**
give a summary	**outline**
sum up	**give an outline**

Questions using these phrases ask you to choose an answer that provides a short version of the passage, but complete in its scope.

Read the question carefully. Follow these steps:

Step 1: Check for one of the phrases listed above. Underline it.

Step 2: Circle the part of the reading the question asks about.

Look at how one student, Claudette, went over the question below.

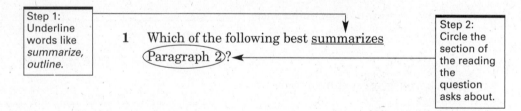

Step 1: Underline words like *summarize, outline.*

1 Which of the following best <u>summarizes</u> Paragraph 2?

Step 2: Circle the section of the reading the question asks about.

A. Read each of the following questions carefully. Underline the phrase that asks you to choose a summary. Circle the section of the reading the question asks about.

1. The passage is best summarized by which of the following?

2. Which statement best outlines Paragraph 5?

3. Which of the following is the best summary of Paragraph 2?

4. The final paragraph is summed up best by which of the following?

Choosing the Best Summary

Reading Section

How do I answer it?

Step 1: Underline words like *summary or sum up.*

Step 2: Circle the part of the reading the question asks about.

Step 3: Cross out answers that have the wrong information.

Step 4: Cross out the answers that leave out major points from the passage.

Step 5: Go back to the passage. Underline one sentence in each paragraph that gives the main idea. If the passage is only one paragraph, underline the subject and verb of each sentence in it.

Step 6: Read your answer choices carefully. Choose the answer that best gives all the information you underlined.

> **TIP**
> Remember that the best summary has all the important points of a passage.

Look at the model below. See how one student, Claudette, went through steps 1–5 to answer a question about the passage "Built for Speed."

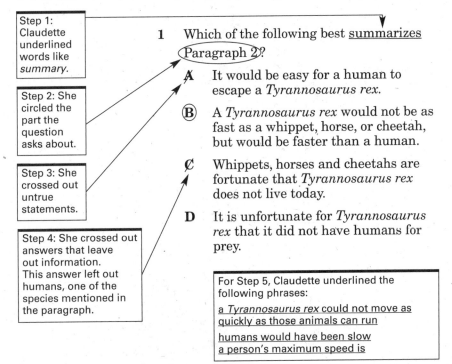

Step 1: Claudette underlined words like *summary.*

Step 2: She circled the part the question asks about.

Step 3: She crossed out untrue statements.

Step 4: She crossed out answers that leave out information. This answer left out humans, one of the species mentioned in the paragraph.

1   Which of the following best <u>summarizes</u> Paragraph 2?

A   It would be easy for a human to escape a *Tyrannosaurus rex.*

Ⓑ   A *Tyrannosaurus rex* would not be as fast as a whippet, horse, or cheetah, but would be faster than a human.

C   Whippets, horses and cheetahs are fortunate that *Tyrannosaurus rex* does not live today.

D   It is unfortunate for *Tyrannosaurus rex* that it did not have humans for prey.

For Step 5, Claudette underlined the following phrases:

a *Tyrannosaurus rex* could not move as quickly as those animals can run

humans would have been slow

a person's maximum speed is

For Step 6, Claudette chose B. Since she had underlined "a Tyrannosaurus rex," "those animals," "humans," and "a person's," she knew that the answer had to include all of those points.

Choosing the Best Summary

Reading Section

Practice Your Skills

> **REMEMBER!**
>
> √ Read the question. Underline words like *summarize* and *outline*.
> √ Circle the part the question asks about.
> √ Cross out answers that have wrong information.
> √ Cross out answers that leave out information.
>
> √ Underline the subject and verb in each sentence of a paragraph or the main sentence in each paragraph of a section.
> √ Choose the answer that includes all the underlined information.

The following questions refer to the passage "Built for Speed." Read each one and choose your answer. Copy the information from the reading that supports each answer in the spaces next to each question.

1   The passage is best summarized by which of the following?

  A   Whippets, horses, cheetahs, and humans run faster than a Tyrannosaurus rex would.

  B   Whippets, horses, and cheetahs run faster than humans because they have four legs.

  C   Physical features determine an animal's maximum speed.

  D   Leg length determines speed.

SUPPORTING INFORMATION:

_____

_____

_____

_____

2   Which statement best outlines Paragraph 3?

  F   Whippets, horses, and cheetahs run on four legs.

  G   Biped mammals cannot run as fast as quadruped mammals because two of their limbs are not used for running.

  H   Quadrupeds run faster than humans because they have four limbs.

  J   Quadrupeds use all four limbs for running.

SUPPORTING INFORMATION:

_____

_____

_____

_____

3   The final paragraph is summed up best by which of the following?

  A   It is most useful for animals to have both speed and endurance.

  B   A *Tyrannosaurus rex* could never catch a cheetah.

  C   Quadrupeds have better endurance than bipeds.

  D   Cheetahs have poor endurance.

SUPPORTING INFORMATION:

_____

_____

_____

_____

Let's Clean Up Sherwood Forest

Reading Section

Dear Ms. Baker:

Because you are the faculty sponsor of the Evansville High School Beta Club, I am writing to suggest a service project for our club to organize and run this spring: a community cleanup of Sherwood Forest, the wooded area behind our school campus.

Even before I attended Evansville High School, I noticed the litter in Sherwood Forest. As a child I picnicked there with my family, and I remember seeing plenty of garbage, including soda cans stuck on the ends of tree branches. Once I even saw a family toss plastic bags and cups under a pine tree upon finishing their meal, as if that were the same as throwing them in a trash can. More recently, I was sorry to see some of our students having garbage-pitching contests there. These disrespectful students filled their lunch bags with rocks and hurled them as far as they could into the woods.

This kind of irresponsible behavior certainly damages the appearance of the woods. I can see the litter from as far away as the classrooms on the south side of the school, and it doesn't make me want to spend time in the forest. In addition to being ugly, litter also creates danger for the animals that live in Sherwood Forest. Animals can cut themselves on aluminum can openings or get stuck in plastic bags and suffocate.

By talking to Jane Maxwell, the president of a local environmentalist group, I learned that the litter problem in Sherwood Forest is worse now than it probably ever has been. By studying certain sections of the woods over time, Ms. Maxwell and her group have discovered that the amount of litter in Sherwood Forest has increased dramatically over the past ten years. It seems as if people have forgotten what Sherwood Forest should be: a quiet place to walk, think, and enjoy nature.

It makes sense for the Beta Club to clean up Sherwood Forest. It is right in our own backyard, so the way it looks reflects on our school and student body. In addition to cleaning up litter, we could raise money to get trash cans placed at the ends of the trails, and we could talk to city officials to get those cans emptied regularly. The cleanup effort could also mark the start of an educational plan to let others in the community and in our school know that we value the forest and we don't want people littering it in the future. Please consider presenting this idea for a service project to the members of Evansville High School's Beta Club.

Sincerely,
Sasha Sidoryansky

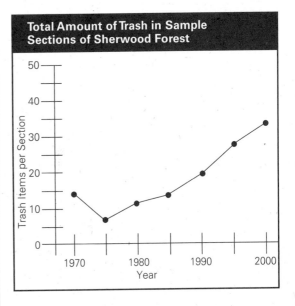

Total Amount of Trash in Sample Sections of Sherwood Forest

Name _____   Date _____

Choosing Facts

What's the question?

Some questions ask you to decide which answer is a fact from the reading. Here is an example of one of these questions.

1 Which is a FACT from this passage?

A People who litter in Sherwood Forest are responsible.

B Cleaning up Sherwood Forest seems to be the best project for the Beta Club.

C The amount of litter in Sherwood Forest has increased over the past ten years.

D Sherwood Forest should be preserved as a place to walk and enjoy nature.

These questions ask you to choose an answer that is not making a judgment or expressing an opinion. You should only choose an answer if it makes a statement that you can prove.

> **TIP**
> When the word EXCEPT is in the question, look for the one answer that is different—that is, find the fact among the opinions or the one opinion among the facts.

Read the question carefully. Follow these steps:

Step 1: Circle the word *FACT* or *FACTS*.

Step 2: Underline what the question is asking about.

Step 3: If the word EXCEPT is in the question, underline it twice.

Look at how one student, Ana, went over the question below.

Step 1: Ana circled the word *FACTS*.

2 All of the following are (FACTS) about Evansville High School EXCEPT—

Step 2: She underlined what the question was asking about.

Step 3: She underlined *EXCEPT* twice.

A. Read each of the following questions carefully. Circle the words *FACTS* or *FACT*. Underline the focus of the fact. Underline the word *EXCEPT* twice.

1. Which is a FACT from this passage?

2. All of these are FACTS from the passage EXCEPT—

3. Which is a FACT about the Beta Club?

4. All of the following are FACTS about Sherwood Forest EXCEPT—

Choosing Facts

How do I answer it?

Step 1: Circle the word *FACT* or *FACTS*.

Step 2: Underline what the question is asking about. If the word EXCEPT is in the question, underline it twice. In this case, remember to look for the answer that is NOT a fact.

Step 3: Look at the answers. If you are looking for a fact, cross out answers with *should, think, feel, believe, seems,* or *probably*—these words signal an opinion.

Step 4: Cross out answers that are not true or that have information not mentioned in the reading.

Step 5: Underline phrases in the reading that are about the question's subject.

Step 6: Choose the answer you think is right. Make certain its information can be proven true or false.

Look at the model below. See how one student, Ana, went through steps 1–6 to answer a question about the passage "Let's Clean Up Sherwood Forest."

Step 1: She circled the word *FACTS.*

Step 2: Ana underlined what the question was asking about. She underlined the word *EXCEPT* twice.

Steps 3 and 4: Ana was looking for an opinion, so she looked for opinion words in the answers.

1   All of the following are (FACTS) about Evansville High School EXCEPT—

A   Ms. Baker is the faculty sponsor of the Beta Club.

B   Sherwood Forest is behind the school campus.

(C)   Irresponsible teachers on campus (probably) littered Sherwood Forest.

D   Evansville High School has a Beta Club.

For Step 5, Ana underlined the following phrases about Evansville High School:

... you are the faculty sponsor of the Evansville High School Beta Club ...

... Sherwood Forest, the wooded area behind our school campus.

For Step 6, Ana chose **C** and marked it on her answer sheet. The word *EXCEPT* in the question meant that Ana had to choose the statement that was NOT a fact. Since **C** had information *not* in the reading and included the word *probably,* it was not a fact.

Choosing Facts

Reading Section

Practice Your Skills

> **REMEMBER!**
>
> √ Circle the word *FACT* or *FACTS*. Underline the focus. Underline *EXCEPT* twice.
>
> √ Check for answers that have opinion words. Cross out those answers.
>
> √ Cross out answers that are not true or that have information not mentioned.
>
> √ Underline phrases that make statements about the question's focus.
>
> √ Choose your answer and make sure you can prove it.

The following questions refer to the passage "Let's Clean Up Sherwood Forest."
Read each one and choose your answer. Copy the statements you find about each
question's main focus into the spaces next to each question.

1   Which is a FACT from this passage?

   A   People who litter in Sherwood Forest are responsible.

   B   Cleaning up Sherwood Forest seems to be the best project for the Beta Club.

   C   The amount of litter in Sherwood Forest has increased over the past ten years.

   D   Sherwood Forest should be preserved as a place to walk and enjoy nature.

STATEMENTS:

_____

_____

_____

_____

2   All of these are FACTS from the passage EXCEPT—

   F   Litter can be seen from the south side of the school.

   G   It seems people have forgotten that the forest is a place to enjoy nature.

   H   There has been litter in Sherwood Forest for over 25 years.

   J   Jane Maxwell is the president of a local environmentalist group.

STATEMENTS:

_____

_____

_____

3   Which is a FACT about the Beta Club?

   A   The Beta Club is a group from Evansville High School.

   B   The club is looking for a service project.

   C   Cleaning the forest would be a good project for the club.

   D   The club should place trash cans in the forest.

STATEMENTS:

_____

_____

_____

Choosing Opinions   *Reading Section*

What's the question?

Some questions ask you to decide which answer is an opinion from the reading.
Here is an example of one of these questions.

1   Which of the following is an OPINION
     expressed in the passage?

     A   People who litter in Sherwood Forest
          are responsible.

     B   Cleaning up Sherwood Forest is the
          best service project for the Beta Club.

     C   The amount of litter in Sherwood
          Forest has increased over the past
          ten years.

     D   Sherwood Forest should be a place to
          walk and enjoy nature.

An opinion is a personal idea or belief, such as "Dogs are better than cats." An
opinion can't be proven with numbers or facts.

> **TIP**
>
> Questions that have the following wording are also asking you to
> choose an opinion:
> All of the following are FACTS from the passage EXCEPT—
>
> **Instead of circling the word *OPINION*, circle the words *FACTS*
> and *EXCEPT*.**

Read the question carefully. Follow these steps:

Step 1: Circle the word OPINION.

Step 2: Underline any words that tell what the opinion will be about.

Look at how one student, Manuel, went over the question below.

| Step 1: Circle the word *OPINION*. | 1.   Which of the following is an OPINION about the Beta Club? | Step 2: Manuel underlined words that tell what the opinion will be about. |

A. Read each of the following questions carefully. Circle the word *OPINION*.
   Underline words that tell what the opinion will be about.

1. Which of the following statements from the passage is an OPINION?

2. Which statement is an OPINION?

3. Which is an OPINION expressed in the passage?

4. Which statement is an OPINION about Sherwood Forest?

Choosing Opinions

How do I answer it?

Step 1: Circle the word OPINION. Underline words that tell what the opinion is about.

Step 2: Cross out answers that you can prove.

Step 3: Cross out answers that are not true or that have information not mentioned in the reading.

Step 4: Circle words like *should, think, feel, believe, seems, probably.* These words signal an opinion.

Step 5: Underline phrases in the reading passage that show the opinion.

Step 6: Choose your answer. Try saying your answer using, "I think that..." to be sure it's an opinion. Is it about the right part of the passage?

Look at the model below. See how Manuel went through steps 1–6 to answer a question about the passage "Let's Clean Up Sherwood Forest."

Step 1: Circle the word *OPINION.* Underline what the opinion will be about.

Step 2: Manuel crossed out answer **A,** since you could easily prove whether the forest is behind the school or not.

Step 3: Manuel crossed out answer **C,** since this information is not in the reading.

1 Which idea from the passage is an OPINION about Evansville High School?

A Sherwood Forest is behind the school campus.

B Sherwood Forest should be a place to enjoy nature.

C Irresponsible teachers on campus probably littered Sherwood Forest.

D The school's Beta Club should organize a community cleanup.

Step 4: He circled the opinion word *should* in answers **B** and **D.**

For step 5, Manuel looked for phrases to support choices **B** and **D** in the reading. He didn't find anything to support choice **B,** but he underlined this to support choice **D:**

It makes sense for the Beta Club to clean up Sherwood Forest.

For step 6, Manuel chose **D.** He said, "I think that the school's Beta Club should organize a community cleanup." The choice was an opinion and it was expressed in the passage, so he knew his answer was right.

Choosing Opinions

Practice Your Skills

> **REMEMBER!**
>
> √ Circle the word *OPINION*. Underline words that tell what opinion to look for.
>
> √ Cross out answers that are not true or that have information not mentioned.
>
> √ Cross out answers that have statements you can prove.
>
> √ Circle opinion words in the remaining answers.
>
> √ Underline phrases in the reading that show the opinion being expressed.
>
> √ Choose and check your answer.

The following questions refer to the passage "Let's Clean Up Sherwood Forest."
Read each one and choose your answer.

1 Which of the following is an OPINION expressed in the passage?
  A People who litter in Sherwood Forest are responsible.
  B Cleaning up Sherwood Forest is the best service project for the Beta Club.
  C The amount of litter in Sherwood Forest has increased over the past ten years.
  D Sherwood Forest should be a place to walk and enjoy nature.

CHECK YOUR ANSWER:

Is it an opinion?   ❏

Is it about the right part of the passage? ❏

Is the information included in the passage? ❏

2 Which statement is an OPINION?
  F Students hurled lunch bags full of rocks into the forest.
  G It makes sense for the Beta Club to clean up Sherwood Forest.
  H An environmentalist group has measured the trash in Sherwood Forest.
  J The writer saw litter in the forest when she was a child.

CHECK YOUR ANSWER:

Is it an opinion?   ❏

Is it about the right part of the passage? ❏

Is the information included in the passage? ❏

3 Which is an OPINION about the Beta Club?
  A The Beta Club is a group from Evansville High School.
  B The club is looking for a service project.
  C Cleaning the forest would be a good community project.
  D The club should place trash cans in the forest.

CHECK YOUR ANSWER:

Is it an opinion?   ❏

Is it about the right part of the passage? ❏

Is the information included in the passage? ❏

TAKING THE TEST

The Elimination Process

How do I choose the best answer?

When you take a test, you will probably have to choose among four or five answer choices. Sometimes you might have to choose an answer that you're not sure of. By using the process of elimination, or crossing out answers you're pretty sure are wrong, you can make a better guess at the right answer.

The best way to be ready for the test is, of course, to practice answering each type of question. However, these tips will also help you narrow down your answer choices:

Writing Section

- When in doubt, trust your first impulses. You probably know more than you think you know.
- Read every word of the question twice.
- Circle what the question is asking about.
- After reading the question, cross out two answers that you are pretty sure are wrong.
- For grammar, decide if the question is about a noun or a verb, or if it is about punctuation.
- Remember that each sentence needs to have a subject and a verb
- If you are trying to decide between two answers, talk it out. Instead of saying, "I think this should be capitalized," give the rule that tells why: "The names of cities and countries are supposed to be capitalized.

Reading Section

- As you read the passage, remember that you don't have to understand every word to get the gist, or main idea.
- Underline what the question is asking you to do, such as make an inference or choose a fact. Cross out any answer choices that don't do those things.
- Cross out answers that you can't underline phrases to support in the reading.
- Cross out answers that aren't true or aren't mentioned in the reading.
- Give reasons for your answer. You should be able to underline phrases in the reading to prove your answer is right.
- Trust your first impulses. You probably know more than you think you know.

The Elimination Process

Taking the Test

List Your Skills

As you complete each section of this book, write tips that best help you answer each kind of question in the chart below.

Type of Question	My Strategy
Sentence Completion	
Error Identification	
Revision in Context	
Analogies	
Synonyms and Antonyms	
Reading Context Clues	
Reading Background Knowledge	
Finding Supporting Evidence	
Determining Purpose	
Making Inferences and Predictions	
Choosing the Main Idea	
Choosing the best Summary	
Choosing Facts/Opinions	

Pacing

How long do I take for each section?

Knowing how much time that you spend on each test question is called **pacing**. You want to give yourself enough time to answer a question well. It's important, however, that you don't let a question take up too much time.

These pacing strategies might help you make the most of your time during the test:

Before the Test:

- Find out if you can choose what section to do first, or if you have to do them in a particular order.
- If you can pick the order in which you will do the test, do the easiest sections first.
- Know the instructions for each section of the test. Read the instructions on practice tests. Discuss them with your teacher to be sure you understand exactly what you're supposed to do.
- Take practice tests. Figure out how long you usually spend on each type of question.
- Time yourself so you know how much time you need for each section.

On Test Day:

- Be sure to get at least eight hours of sleep the night before.
- Eat a healthy breakfast. Avoid drinks with caffeine, such as sodas and coffee, which can break your concentration during the test.
- Always read the directions carefully before you begin each section. You want to be sure of what you are doing.
- Answer the easy questions first.
- As you read the reading passages, underline key ideas so you'll be able to find them later. Circle any important words you don't understand, and then use context clues to figure out their meaning.
- If you come across a word you don't know, don't panic. Circle the part of the word that you recognize. Try to guess the meaning from the sentences before and after.
- If a question takes twice the amount of time that you normally need, circle it. Skip it for now and come back to it later.
- When working on an essay question, allow yourself 7 minutes to organize your essay, 20 minutes to write it and revise it, and 3 minutes for editing.
- If you have any time left, use it to check your answers.

Answer Key *(Answers for pages 60–114 can be found on page 116)*

p. 2: **1A 2G 3B 4F**

p. 4: **1A** It's the only one that sounds right. **2F** All verbs in selection are in present tense. **3D** The pronoun is replacing "pitcher" from previous sentence.

p. 5: **1B 2F 3C 4J**

p. 7: **1C** The comma doesn't break the sentence where it's supposed to. **2F** The word "revisits" has an extra letter. **3B** "Night Club" is not a proper noun, so it shouldn't be capitalized. **4J** The spelling is correct, and the commas break the sentence where they're supposed to.

p. 11: **1D** No commas are needed. **2G** "Especially the women" is a fragment. Combine it with the sentence before. **3C** Run-on sentence—add *because* and a comma. **4H** Two short sentences need to be combined. **5A** Fragment needs a subject and verb.

p. 15: **1D** A directory is made up of names just like an almanac is made up of information. **2A** A flower is aromatic just like a puzzle is enigmatic (mysterious). **3A** A basket is made of reeds just like music is made of notes. **4E** A cure ends a disease just like a resolution ends a dilemma.

p. 18: **1B 2B 3A 4B 5E**

p. 22: Possible responses:
1. "diverse" means "people from many different areas" **2.** "pattern of settlement" means each group had its own way of living **3.** "lacking" means not having the skills to find work **4.** "mobilized" means taking action

p. 23: Possible responses:
1. (1) Smoking is bad for your health. (2) It is difficult to quit smoking. **2.** (1) School all year would be hard. (2) More vacations during the year would be good. **3.** (1) My cat is hard to train. (2) My friend's dog will heel on command.

p. 24: Possible responses:
1. separate **2.** change of government **3.** look for family history

p. 27: **2.** The author hints that Murasaki— **3.** The reading proves that Murasaki—

p. 29: **1B** "In tenth-century Japan, girls were neither valued nor expected to excel in school." ". . . Many people thought women were not smart enough to learn such skills." **2J** "She avoided social life in the palace, even during cold winters." **3B** "Many contemporary scholars believe that she wrote the first and oldest novel in human history—*The Tale of Genji*." "Murasaki's novel revolutionized literature." "Some of her writing techniques were so advanced that they were not used again in literature for hundreds of years."

p. 30: **2.** The main point of the second sentence of the closing paragraph is to— ¶10 **3.** This

essay is saying that— ¶all **4.** The main purpose of the final paragraph is to— ¶10 **5.** The author wrote the initial paragraph in order to— ¶1

p. 32: **1A** "Despite her father's and society's disapproval, Murasaki was determined to be a writer." **2H** "Murasaki simplified her life so that she could devote most of her attention and energy to writing." "She avoided social life in the palace, even during cold winters." **3D** "Murasaki's devotion to writing paid off, although her accomplishments were not recognized for centuries." "Many contemporary scholars believe that she wrote the first and oldest novel in human history."

p. 34: **2.** The alliance with Texcoco and Tlacopan gives one reason to believe— **3.** From Montezuma's actions you can tell that— **4.** From the empire's wealth, you can infer that— **5.** According to the author, one can tell that—

p. 36: **1A** "fierce and ambitious" "They found paid work as soldiers for local rulers." **2H** "This group of cities became the leading power in the Valley of Mexico." ". . . the alliance controlled the huge area that stretched from central Mexico to the Atlantic and Pacific coasts. . . ." **3C** "Under Montezuma, the Aztec empire began to weaken." ". . . the emperor demanded even more tribute and sacrifices. Some provinces revolted."

p. 37: **1.** In the future the Aztecs' empire will most likely— **2.** You can tell from the passage that the Spanish will probably not— **3.** What will Montezuma be least likely to do next? **4.** Which of the following is likely to happen after the Spanish arrive?

p. 39: **1A** "The people were unhappy with the cruel and demanding Aztecs." "a period of instability and unrest" **2J** ". . . in addition to the problems at home, another threat appeared: the arrival of the Spanish." **3B** "For nearly a century, the Aztecs had been demanding tribute and sacrifices from the provinces."

p. 41: **1.** The first paragraph evaluates— **2.** Which statement best expresses the main idea in Paragraph 5? **3.** According to the third paragraph, biped mammals— **4.** The main idea of the final paragraph—

p. 43: **1D** "This ability to attain a high running speed is not as useful as it might seem." ". . . if a slow but determined *Tyrannosaurus rex* had encountered a modern-day cheetah, that dinosaur could have caught the fastest mammal on Earth." **2H** ". . . a *Tyrannosaurus rex* could not move as quickly as a modern-day whippet . . . , horse, or cheetah." "People cannot achieve the high speeds of quadrupeds.

. . ." **3C** "People cannot achieve the high speeds of quadrupeds . . . because two of their limbs, the arms, are hanging uselessly at their sides."

p. 44: **1.** The passage is best summarized by which of the following? **2.** Which statement best outlines Paragraph 5? **3.** Which of the following is the best summary of Paragraph 2? **4.** The final paragraph is summed up best by which of the following?

p. 46: **1C** "This huge creature could achieve such high speeds because it had unusually large thigh muscles." "Horses are quadrupeds that can use all four limbs when running, which enables a maximum speed almost twice as fast as that of human beings." "Cheetahs . . . have hip joints and shoulder blades that move easily." **2G** "People cannot achieve the high speeds of quadrupeds . . . because two of their limbs, the arms, are hanging uselessly at their sides." **3A** "Consequently, if a slow but determined *Tyrannosaurus rex* had encountered a modern-day cheetah, that dinosaur could have caught the fastest mammal on earth."

p. 48: **1.** Which is a FACT from this passage? **2.** All of these are FACTS from the passage EXCEPT— **3.** Which is a FACT about the Beta Club? **4.** All of the following are FACTS about Sherwood Forest EXCEPT—

p. 50: **1C** "By studying certain sections of the woods over time, Ms. Maxwell and her group have discovered that the amount of litter in Sherwood Forest has increased dramatically over the past ten years." **2G** ". . . I remember seeing plenty of garbage, including soda cans stuck on the ends of tree branches." "It seems as if people have forgotten what Sherwood Forest should be: a quiet place to walk, think, and enjoy nature." **3A** ". . . you are the faculty sponsor of the Evansville High School Beta Club." "It makes sense for the Beta Club to clean up Sherwood Forest." "Please consider presenting this idea for a service project to the members of Evansville High School's Beta Club."

p. 51: **1.** Which of the following statements from the passage is an OPINION? **2.** Which statement is an OPINION? **3.** Which is an OPINION expressed in the passage? **4.** Which statement is an OPINION about Sherwood Forest?

p. 53: **1D 2G 3D**

p. 56: Students should write the strategies that they find most helpful. The "Remember" boxes in the lessons provide a good source for succinctly worded strategies.

SECCIÓN DE ESCRITURA:
¿Cuál es la pregunta y cómo la respondo?

¿Como completar una oración?   *Sección de escritura*

¿Cuál es la pregunta?

En algunas preguntas se te pide que elijas una palabra o frase gramaticalmente correcta para **completar la oración.** Las instrucciones son de este tipo:

Read the passage and choose the word or group of words that belongs in each space. Mark the letter for your answer.

Las preguntas son como las que se indican a continuación:

Deberás elegir **la forma y el tiempo verbal** correctos.	Our vacation to California this summer was the best trip I have ever __(1)__ . We went to the city my father lived in when he was a boy, and it was the __(2)__ we had ever seen. My sister wanted to stay at the playground, but I __(3)__ want to go. I wanted to go to the beach. Eventually __(4)__ reached a compromise, and we went to both places.

En este caso, tendrás que elegir **la forma correcta de un adjetivo.**	

También deberás estar preparado para usar correctamente las formas afirmativas y negativas.

A menudo se te pedirá que elijas el pronombre correcto.

1 A taken
   B took
   C been taking
   D had taken

3 A did
   B didn't
   C not didn't
   D not gone

2 F pleasant
   G most pleasant
   H more pleasant
   J most pleasantest

4 F she and I
   G she and me
   H me and her
   J her and I

SUGERENCIA

Dado que en muchas preguntas se te pide que elijas la forma o el tiempo verbal correcto, subraya todos los verbos y traza un círculo alrededor de todos los sujetos a medida que leas el párrafo.

SPANISH

Cómo completar una oración

Sección de escritura

¿Cómo contesto la pregunta?

Paso 1. Lee el pasaje. Subraya los verbos principales del párrafo. Traza un círculo alrededor de cada sujeto.

Paso 2. Lee las respuestas correspondientes a la primera pregunta. Lee la oración que está antes y después de la pregunta.

Paso 3. Tacha dos respuestas que creas casi con certeza que están equivocadas.

Paso 4. Para que te sea más fácil elegir entre las dos respuestas restantes, te ofrecemos las siguientes sugerencias:

- Para las preguntas sobre **verbos,** traza un círculo alrededor del sujeto de la oración. Subraya el verbo en las oraciones anterior y posterior. Elige la respuesta que concuerde con el sujeto y con el tiempo verbal.

- Para las preguntas sobre **pronombres,** lee las oraciones anterior y posterior. Traza un círculo alrededor de la persona o cosa que el pronombre está reemplazando.

- Para las preguntas **negativas,** tacha las respuestas que tienen doble negativo.

- Para las preguntas sobre **adjetivos,** busca pistas tales como *than* (utilízalo como comparativo, como por ejemplo, *nicer*) o fíjate en las palabras *the* antes del espacio en blanco (utiliza el superlativo, como por ejemplo, *the best singer*).

Paso 5. Elige tu respuesta. Recuerda que deberás dar una razón que justifique que es la mejor respuesta.

Paso 6. Di la oración para tus adentros, incluyendo la respuesta que elegiste. Repítela dos o tres veces.

Mira el modelo que figura a continuación. Observa cómo un estudiante, Eric, cumplió con los pasos del 1 al 6 para completar el ejercicio.

Paso 1. Subraya los verbos principales y traza un círculo alrededor de cada sujeto.	Our (vacation) to California this summer <u>was</u> the best trip I <u>have</u> ever __(1)__. (We) <u>went</u> to the city my father lived in when he was a boy, and (it) <u>was</u> the __(2)__ we had ever seen.	Para el paso 6, Eric leyó la oración dos veces y decidió que su respuesta era la correcta.

Para el paso 2, él leyó las otras oraciones.

1 (A) taken ←
   B took
   Ȼ been taking
   Ð had taken

Para el paso 3. Tacha dos respuestas que creas casi con certeza que están equivocadas.

Para el paso 5, Eric eligió **A.** En el texto, la persona se refiere a un viaje ya realizado que todavía es importante para ella en el presente. Debe usar el presente perfecto. Forma el presente perfecto con el verbo *have,* y el participio pasado del verbo principal, en este caso, *take.*

Para el paso 4, Eric observó los verbos subrayados de las oraciones que preceden la pregunta: *was, have.* Comprendió que la respuesta se refería tanto al pasado como al presente. Luego, observó el sujeto de la oración: *I.*

Cómo completar una oración   *Sección de escritura*

Pon en práctica tus conocimientos

¡RECUERDA!

√ Subraya los verbos y traza un círculo alrededor de los sujetos.

√ Lee las oraciones que se encuentran antes y después de la pregunta.

√ Tacha dos respuestas que creas casi con certeza que están equivocadas.

√ Busca las pistas que figuran en la oración.

√ Elige una respuesta y explica las razones de tu elección.

√ Repite varias veces la oración, con tu respuesta incluida.

Ahora, sigue estas reglas para contestar las respuestas que figuran a continuación. Al lado de cada pregunta, explica por qué consideras que tu respuesta es correcta.

Read the passage and choose the word or group of words that belongs in each space. Mark the letter for your answer.

Some people complain that baseball is a game that __(1)__ move fast. Yet consider what the batter sees before the pitcher releases the ball. The pitcher __(2)__ on the mound, leaning toward home plate. __(3)__ watches the catcher give the sign for the pitch.

---

1   A   doesn't

    B   doesn't never

    C   hardly doesn't

    D   does not scarcely

Motivo por el cual mi respuesta es correcta:

_____

_____

_____

2   F   stands

    G   stood

    H   has stood

    J   was standing

Motivo por el cual mi respuesta es correcta:

_____

_____

_____

3   A   I

    B   It

    C   They

    D   He

Motivo por el cual mi respuesta es correcta:

_____

_____

_____

SPANISH

Identificación de errores

Sección de escritura

¿Cuál es la pregunta?

Hay preguntas en las que se te pedirá que **indiques los errores** o que digas qué es lo que está equivocado en una oración.

Por lo general, estos errores son de **ortografía, puntuación** o de **uso de mayúsculas.**

Las instrucciones de la prueba son de este tipo:

Read the passage and decide which type of error, if any, appears in each underlined section. Mark the letter for your answer.

Las preguntas son como las que se indican a continuación:

Se te pedirá que encuentres errores en el **uso de las mayúsculas.** Pon mayúscula a nombres de lugares, personas y puestos de trabajo específicos, así como a la primera palabra de cada oración.	All ladies apparel is on sale now to celebrate the opening of our new store in <u>cisco</u>. ➤ **(1)** With every purchase of $50.00 or more, <u>customers will receive</u> **(2)** ◀ a <u>specal scarf in blue or black</u>. We are also giving away a free weekend <u>trip for two; so ask for</u> details when you come in. **(3)** ◀ <u>Act now</u>! **(4)**

Aquí debes encontrar un **error de puntuación.**

También deberás reconocer cuando la respuesta no tiene **ningún error.**

Deberás estar atento para encontrar los **errores de ortografía.**

1	**A**	Spelling error
	B	Capitalization error
	C	Punctuation error
	D	No error
2	**F**	Spelling error
	G	Capitalization error
	H	Punctuation error
	J	No error

3	**A**	Spelling error
	B	Capitalization error
	C	Punctuation error
	D	No error
4	**F**	Spelling error
	G	Capitalization error
	H	Punctuation error
	J	No error

SUGERENCIA

Pregúntate lo siguiente:

- **Ortografía:** ¿A las palabras subrayadas les falta alguna letra?
- **Uso de mayúsculas:** ¿Los nombres propios están con mayúscula? ¿La primera palabra de cada oración está escrita con mayúscula?
- **Puntuación:** ¿Las oraciones tienen puntos finales y signos de interrogación al final? ¿Hay comas antes de las palabras como *and, but* o *for, so* y *yet*? ¿Hay comas antes de los ítems de una lista? ¿Hay comas antes de los apositivos (frases que describen a alguien), como por ejemplo, *"John, the baseball player, is there"*?

SPANISH

Identificación de errores

¿Cómo la respondo?

Paso 1. Tómate unos instantes para leer el pasaje. Es posible que haya palabras que nunca viste antes, como por ejemplo, nombres de lugares. Utiliza el resto de la oración (el contexto) para comprender el significado.

Paso 2. Lee la sección subrayada de cada oración. Determina a qué categoría gramatical pertenece cada palabra. ¿Es un sustantivo, un verbo, un adjetivo o un adverbio?

Paso 3. Tacha dos respuestas que creas casi con certeza que están equivocadas.

Paso 4. Para elegir entre las dos respuestas restantes, te ofrecemos las siguientes sugerencias:

- Busca los **errores ortográficos.** A las palabras tal vez les falte o les sobre una letra.

- Busca errores en el **uso de las mayúsculas.** Traza un círculo alrededor de los sustantivos en una oración. ¿Se trata de nombres propios o de sustantivos comunes?

- Analiza las **normas de puntuación** en la frase subrayada. Traza un círculo alrededor de las palabras que se encuentran antes y después de los puntos, comas u otros signos de puntuación. ¿El signo de puntuación separa las palabras o las oraciones donde corresponde?

- Recuerda, solamente unas pocas preguntas tienen por respuesta correcta **Ningún error.** Observa atentamente las oraciones antes de elegir dicha respuesta.

Paso 5. Elige la mejor respuesta y explica por qué la elegiste.

Mira el ejemplo que figura a continuación. Observa cómo Elena cumplió con los pasos 1 a 5 para identificar el error en la pregunta.

noun

Paso 1. Elena leyó el pasaje y se dio cuenta de que *cisco* es un lugar.

All ladies apparel is on sale now to celebrate the opening of our

new store in (cisco). With every purchase of $50.00 or more,
(1)

Paso 2. Elena decidió que *cisco* es un nombre porque es un lugar.

customers will receive a specal scarf in blue or black. We are also
(2)

giving away a free weekend trip for two; so ask for details when
(3)

you come in. Act now!
(4)

Paso 3. Elena comprendió que el punto estaba correctamente colocado, por lo cual descartó las opciones C y D.

1 **A** Spelling error

   (B) Capitalization error

   C Punctuation error

   D No error

Paso 5. Elena eligió **B**. Para justificar su elección, dijo que probablemente *cisco* era una ciudad y que los nombres de cualquier ciudad se escriben con su primera letra en mayúscula.

Para el paso 4, Elena pensó que *cisco* era el nombre de una ciudad, es decir, un nombre propio. No estaba segura respecto a cómo se deletreaba, pero sabía que tenía que comenzar con una mayúscula.

Identificación de errores

Sección de escritura

Pon en práctica tus conocimientos

SUGERENCIA

√ Lee todo el pasaje y busca pistas en el contexto que te ayuden a comprender las palabras que no conozcas.

√ Decide si las palabras subrayadas son sustantivos, verbos, adjetivos o adverbios.

√ Descarta las respuestas que creas casi con certeza que están equivocadas.

√ Busca palabras que te den pistas acerca de cuál es la puntuación correcta.

√ Busca en sustantivos errores en el uso de las mayúsculas.

√ Observa atentamente las palabras para determinar si les faltan o les sobran letras.

√ Elige una respuesta y explica por qué.

Movies and television <u>can't compete, with</u> the reader's ability to fly away to King's Arthur's
　　　　　　　　　　　　　　(1)

court, explore the dingy streets of Charles Dicken's London, or laugh with Amy Tan when

she <u>revisites the crazy</u> world of her mother in *The Joy Luck Club*. Reading also keeps us
　　　　(2)

abreast of the world around us, from Sammy Sosa's latest homerun to the best new

<u>Night Club</u> in town. <u>In addition, of course,</u> books can be read again and again.
　(3)　　　　　　　　　(4)

1　**A**　Spelling error

　　B　Capitalization error

　　C　Punctuation error

　　D　No error

Motivo por el cual mi respuesta es correcta:

_____

_____

_____

2　**F**　Spelling error

　　G　Capitalization error

　　H　Punctuation error

　　J　No error

Motivo por el cual mi respuesta es correcta:

_____

_____

_____

3　**A**　Spelling error

　　B　Capitalization error

　　C　Punctuation error

　　D　No error

Motivo por el cual mi respuesta es correcta:

_____

_____

_____

4　**F**　Spelling error

　　G　Capitalization error

　　H　Punctuation error

　　J　No error

Motivo por el cual mi respuesta es correcta:

_____

_____

_____

SPANISH

Name _____   Date _____

Revisión de contexto   *Sección de escritura*

¿Cuál es la pregunta?

En algunas preguntas se te pedirá que encuentres errores en las secciones subrayadas de un pasaje. Deberás elegir el modo correcto de escribir la oración.

En las preguntas se te pide que indiques el modo en que deben construirse las oraciones.

Las instrucciones en la prueba son de este tipo:

Read the passage. Some sections are underlined. The underlined sections may be one of the following:
- **Incomplete sentences**
- **Run-on sentences**
- **Correctly written sentences that should be combined**
- **Correctly written sentences that do not need to be rewritten**

Choose the best way to write each underlined section and mark the letter for your answer. If the underlined section needs no change, mark the choice "Correct as is."

Las preguntas son como las que se indican a continuación:

> Se te pedirá que encuentres **dos oraciones correctas que deben combinarse en una sola.**

Justin was excited when the Explorer's Club received permission to explore a remote cave. <u>It was virtually untouched</u> **(1)** <u>by modern man. That's why he looked forward to seeing the cave.</u> Justin was thrilled by the possibility of discovering ancient cave drawings.

<u>Justin was disappointed after exploring the cave, they had</u> **(2)** <u>found no drawings</u>. Just as the group was about to leave, his flashlight illuminated some letters carved into the wall. The letters read: "Wilkins 1886." <u>Those letters could have been carved by Clyde</u> **(3)** <u>Wilkins. The area's most notorious outlaw, who had evaded capture for years</u>. Could this cave have been his hideout?

> Deberás estar atento para identificar las **oraciones que no están conectadas en forma coherente.**

> Aquí deberás encontrar **oraciones incompletas.**

SUGERENCIA
Traza un círculo alrededor de los fragmentos **antes** de leer las respuestas.

Revisión de contexto

Sección de escritura

¿Cómo la respondo?

Paso 1. Lee el pasaje. Busca el sujeto y el verbo en cada una de las frases subrayadas. Traza un círculo alrededor del sujeto y del verbo de cada frase.

Paso 2. Determina cuál es el problema. ¿Se trata de una oración incompleta? ¿Se trata de una frase que no sigue a otra en forma coherente o ves dos oraciones que tienen que combinarse en una sola? ¿Ya está escrita correctamente? Busca los siguientes problemas:

	Problema	Ejemplo	Cómo resolver el error	Solución
Fragmento	A la oración le falta el sujeto o un verbo.	The area's most notorious outlaw, who had evaded capture for years.	• Agrega un sujeto y/o un verbo. • Combina el fragmento con otra oración.	<u>Those letters could have been carved by Clyde Wilkins</u>, the area's most notorious outlaw, who had evaded capture for years.
Dos oraciones cortas	Hay que combinar dos oraciones cortas.	It was virtually untouched by modern man. That is why he looked forward to seeing the cave.	• Combina las oraciones usando **and, but, or, because** • Combina las oraciones usando **that, who, which**	He looked forward to seeing this cave <u>because</u> it was virtually untouched by modern man.
Oración no conectada en forma coherente	Una oración contiene dos pensamientos o acciones diferentes no conectados coherentemente.	Justin was disappointed after exploring the cave, they had found no drawings.	• Agrega una coma y **and, but,** o **or.** • Combina las oraciones usando **because, since,** etc.	Justin was disappointed after exploring the cave <u>because</u> they had found no drawings.

Paso 3. Antes de leer las respuestas, decide cómo corregirías la oración. Repite tu respuesta.

Paso 4. Tacha dos respuestas que pienses que son absolutamente incorrectas.

Paso 5. Elige la mejor respuesta e indica la razón de tu elección.

Paso 6. Lee tu respuesta. Subraya el sujeto y el verbo. Asegúrate de que se trata de un pensamiento o una acción completa.

> **SUGERENCIA**
>
> A menudo, una oración incoherente contiene *dos* oraciones que expresan pensamientos o acciones *diferentes* sin relación lógica entre sí. Corrige oraciones incorrectas con comas, **and, but** o **or.**
>
> Oración incoherente: I was late for soccer practice, no one noticed.
>
> Corrección: I was late for soccer practice, **but** no one noticed.

SPANISH

Revisión de contexto

Sección de escritura

Mira el modelo que figura a continuación. Observa cómo Yukio cumplió con los pasos del 1 a 6 para contestar una pregunta de revisión de contexto.

Paso 1. Yukio trazó un círculo alrededor del sujeto y de un verbo en cada una de las frases subrayadas.

Paso 2. Yukio determinó que se trataba de dos oraciones que debían combinarse.

Paso 3. Yukio pensó en el modo en que podría combinar las oraciones: "Justin quería ver la caverna porque no había sido tocada por el hombre contemporáneo."

Justin was excited when the Explorer's Club received permission to explore a remote cave. (It was) virtually untouched by modern man. (That's) why he looked forward to seeing the cave.
(1)
Justin was thrilled by the possibility of discovering ancient cave drawings.

Paso 5. Yukio analizó las opciones **B** y **D**. Comprendió que la opción **D** estaba equivocada porque el hombre contemporáneo ya no vive en cavernas. Determinó que la respuesta correcta era **B**.

1 **A** It was virtually untouched by modern man since he looked forward to seeing this cave.

B He looked forward to seeing this cave because it was virtually untouched by modern man.

C It was virtually untouched by modern man, who looked forward to seeing this cave.

D He looked forward to seeing this modern man's cave that was virtually untouched.

Paso 4. Yukio tachó las oraciones que obviamente eran incorrectas.

Paso 6. Yukio subrayó el sujeto y el verbo: "He looked forward to seeing this cave because it was virtually untouched by modern man." Con sus propias palabras, expresó la oración: Justin quería ver la caverna porque nunca había sido tocada por el hombre contemporáneo.

SUGERENCIA

- Intenta combinar las oraciones con tus propias palabras *antes* de leer las respuestas.

- No te preocupes si no entiendes todas las palabras del párrafo. Aún así puedes escoger la respuesta correcta, incluso si, por ejemplo, no sabes lo que significa con exactitud.

SPANISH

Revisión de contexto

Sección de escritura

Pon en práctica tus conocimientos

> **¡RECUERDA!**
>
> √ Lee el pasaje. Traza un círculo alrededor del sujeto y el verbo en cada una de las frases subrayadas.
>
> √ Determina qué tipo de error es: una oración incompleta, una oración conectada en forma incoherente, dos oraciones que deben combinarse en una sola o una oración ya escrita correctamente.
>
> √ Antes de leer las respuestas, decide cómo corregirías la oración.
>
> √ Tacha las respuestas incorrectas.
>
> √ Elige la mejor respuesta e indica la razón de tu elección.
>
> √ Lee tu respuesta. Subraya el sujeto y el verbo. Di en tus propias palabras el pensamiento o acción que expresa la oración.

Ahora sigue estas indicaciones para contestar las siguientes preguntas. Al lado de cada pregunta, escribe por qué tu respuesta es la correcta.

<u>The Academy Awards will be presented on March 23 in Los Angeles</u>. The celebrities are
(1)

growing excited. <u>Famous people are getting ready for the big night</u>. <u>Especially the</u>
(2)

<u>women</u>. The fashion industry is also excited. <u>Many of the top designers offer to make</u>

<u>elaborate gowns for the stars attending the program there is so much interest in the</u>
(3)

<u>event</u>. The media are stirred into action. <u>Photographers arrive early</u>. <u>They come from all</u>
(4)

<u>over the world</u>. Everywhere people watch and read about the big event. <u>To see who is</u>
(5)

<u>wearing the most beautiful or most outrageous outfits</u>.

---

1 **A** The Academy Awards, will be presented, on March 23 in Los Angeles.

    B The Academy Awards will be presented, on March 23 in Los Angeles.

    C The Academy Awards will be presented, on March 23, in Los Angeles.

    D Correct as is

Revisión de contexto

2 **F** Famous people are getting ready for the big night especially the women.

G Famous people, especially the women, are getting ready for the big night.

H Famous people are getting ready for the big night; especially the women.

J Correct as is

3 **A** Many of the top designers offer to make elaborate gowns for the stars attending the program; because there is so much interest in the event.

B Many of the top designers offer to make elaborate gowns for the stars attending the program. Because there is so much interest in the event.

C Many of the top designers offer to make elaborate gowns for the stars attending the program, because there is so much interest in the event.

D Correct as is

4 **F** Photographers arrive early, they come from all over the world.

G Photographers arriving early, they come from all over the world.

H Photographers from all over the world arrive early.

J Correct as is

5 **A** Most of them watch to see who is wearing the most beautiful or outrageous outfits.

B Most of them watch, to see who is wearing the most beautiful or outrageous outfits.

C Most of them watching to see who is wearing the most beautiful or outrageous outfits.

D Correct as is

SPANISH

Analogías

Sección de escritura

¿Cuál es la pregunta?

En algunas preguntas se te pedirá que establezcas **analogías.** Una analogía es una comparación de dos pares de palabras.

Mediante una analogía se determina cómo se relacionan dos cosas, las cuales no tienen por qué ser similares.

Las analogías se escriben del siguiente modo:

giraffe: mammal :: grasshopper: insect

Para leer esta analogía, podrías decir: *"Giraffe* es a *mammal* como *grasshopper* es a *insect".*

O sea, una jirafa es un tipo de mamífero, al igual que un saltamontes es un tipo de insecto.

Las instrucciones de este ejercicio son de este tipo:

Each question below consists of a related pair of words or phrases labeled A through E. Select the pair that <u>best</u> expresses the relationship similar to that expressed in the original pair.

Las preguntas son como las que se indican a continuación:

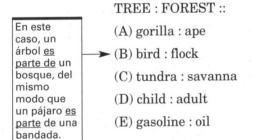

TREE : FOREST ::

En este caso, un árbol <u>es parte de</u> un bosque, del mismo modo que un pájaro <u>es parte</u> de una bandada.

(A) gorilla : ape

(B) bird : flock

(C) tundra : savanna

(D) child : adult

(E) gasoline : oil

Ⓐ ● Ⓒ Ⓓ

Puedes repasar los tipos de relaciones más comúnmente utilizados en las analogías:

VIRUS: DISEASE :: carelessness : error	*Virus* <u>provoca</u> *disease,* del mismo modo que *carelessness* <u>provoca</u> *errors.*
FINGER: HAND :: chip : computer	*Finger* <u>es parte de</u> *hand,* del mismo modo que *chip* <u>es parte de</u> *computer.*
COLD : HOT :: arctic : tropical	*Cold* <u>es lo opuesto de</u> *hot,* del mismo modo que *arctic* <u>es lo opuesto de</u> *tropical.*
CAR : TRANSPORTATION :: phone : communication	*Car* <u>se usa para</u> *transportation,* del mismo modo que *phone* <u>se usa para</u> *communication.*
COMPOSER : SYMPHONY :: architect : building	*Composer* <u>compone</u> *symphony,* del mismo modo que *architect* <u>construye</u> *building.*
OWL : NOCTURNAL :: lion : fierce	*Owl* <u>es, por lo general,</u> *nocturnal,* del mismo modo que *lion* <u>suele ser</u> *fierce.*
ADD : INCREASE :: squander : decrease	*To add* <u>significa lo mismo que</u> *to increase. To squander* <u>significa lo mismo que</u> *to decrease.*
GO : WENT :: lose : lost	*Go* <u>es el tiempo presente de</u> *went,* del mismo modo que *lose* <u>es el tiempo presente de</u> *lost.*

Analogías

¿Cómo la respondo?

Paso 1. Determina la relación entre las dos palabras. Expresa la analogía en forma de oración:

"A tree es parte de a forest".

Paso 2. Analiza las posibles respuestas. Lee cada par de palabras usando la misma frase que usaste con las dos primeras palabras: "A gorilla es parte de an ape". (equivocado)

Paso 3. Descarta las respuestas que no tengan sentido.

Paso 4. Expresa la analogía como una oración completa. *Tree* es parte de *forest,* del mismo modo que *bird* es parte de *flock.* Elige una respuesta.

Paso 5. Si hubiera dos respuestas que consideras que podrían ser correctas, elige una frase diferente. Por ejemplo, "Hay muchísimos trees en forest, del mismo modo que hay muchísimos birds en flock. Decide luego cuál es la mejor opción.

Paso 6. Vuelve a leer la opción que elegiste. Inserta en la oración las palabras de la respuesta: "A bird es parte de flock, del mismo modo que tree es parte de forest."

Mira el modelo que figura a continuación. Observa cómo un estudiante, Mario, cumplió con los pasos del 1 al 6 para contestar una pregunta de analogía:

Para el paso 1, Mario leyó las dos palabras indicadas. Luego dijo la oración: "Un bailiff trabaja en un court".

Paso 3. Mario descartó las opciones **C, D y E.**

10 COURT : BAILIFF::

(A) school : janitor
(B) ranch : foreman ◄
(C) song : singer
(D) senator : congressman
(E) casino : gambler

Para el paso 5, a Mario se le ocurrió una frase diferente en la que incluyó: está a cargo de. Luego leyó A y B con esta nueva oración.

A   Un bailiff está a cargo de un court, del mismo modo que un janitor está a cargo de un school.

B   Un bailiff está a cargo de un court, del mismo modo que un foreman está a cargo de un ranch.

Para los pasos 2 y 3, Mario analizó las posibles respuestas y leyó cada una con la misma frase que utilizó para leer las primeras dos palabras.

A   Un bailiff trabaja en un court, del mismo modo que un janitor trabaja en una school.

B   Un bailiff trabaja en un court, del mismo modo que un foreman trabaja en un ranch.

C   Un bailiff trabaja en un court, del mismo modo que un singer trabaja con un song.

D   Un bailiff trabaja en un court, del mismo modo que un congressman trabaja en un senator.

E   Un bailiff trabaja en un court, del mismo modo que un gambler trabaja en un casino.

Paso 4. A Mario le quedaban las opciones **A y B.** Dijo la analogía y eligió **B.**

Paso 6. Mario decidió que **B** era la respuesta correcta. Cuando volvió a leer la opción elegida, colocó primero su respuesta en la oración: "*Ranch* es a *foreman* como *court* es a *bailiff.*"

SPANISH

Analogías

Sección de escritura

Pon en práctica tus conocimientos

¡RECUERDA!

√ Analiza las dos palabras. Expresa la analogía en forma de oración.

√ Lee cada respuesta usando la misma frase que con las dos primeras palabras.

√ Descarta las respuestas que no tengan sentido.

√ Elige tu respuesta. Di la analogía como una oración completa.

√ Si hubiera dos respuestas que consideras que podrían ser correctas, elige una frase diferente. Decide entonces cuál es la mejor opción.

√ Vuelve a leer la opción que elegiste.

SUGERENCIA

Si no conocieras el significado de una palabra, no te preocupes. Piensa en otras palabras que tengan un significado similar u opuesto a la palabra que sí conoces. Si te resultara útil, escribe varias palabras relacionadas con la palabra que conoces. Tal vez eso te ayude a comprender el significado del término que desconoces.

Ahora sigue los pasos indicados para contestar las preguntas formuladas. Luego de cada pregunta, explica por qué tu respuesta es correcta.

Each question below consists of a related pair of words or phrases labeled A through E. Select the pair that _best_ expresses the relationship similar to that expressed in the original pair.

1 ALMANAC : INFORMATION ::

    (A) plant : flower
    (B) notebook : paper
    (C) woods : bear
    (D) directory : names
    (E) energy : fuel

Motivo por el cual mi respuesta es correcta:

_____
_____
_____
_____
_____

2 PUZZLE : ENIGMATIC ::

    (A) flower : aromatic
    (B) plan : schematic
    (C) satire : requisite
    (D) intuition : rational
    (E) sugar : candy

Motivo por el cual mi respuesta es correcta:

_____
_____
_____
_____
_____

3 MUSIC : NOTES ::

    (A) basket : reeds
    (B) bucket : well
    (C) camera : film
    (D) car : road
    (E) pen : ink

Motivo por el cual mi respuesta es correcta:

_____
_____
_____
_____
_____

4 DILEMMA : RESOLUTION ::

    (A) dialogue : discussion
    (B) evidence : proof
    (C) eyeglasses :
    (D) skepticism : doubt
    (E) disease : cure

Motivo por el cual mi respuesta es correcta:

_____
_____
_____
_____
_____

SPANISH

Sinónimos y antónimos   *Sección de escritura*

¿Cuál es la pregunta?

En algunas preguntas se te pedirá que elijas el **sinónimo** o el **antónimo** de una palabra.

Un **sinónimo** tiene un significado similar.
Un **antónimo** es una palabra que significa lo **opuesto**.

Prueba de sinónimos

Para la prueba de **sinónimos,** las instrucciones son de este tipo:

Decide which word or phrase is most nearly the same in meaning as the word in capital letters. Fill in the circle containing the letter of your answer.

Las preguntas son como las que se indican a continuación:

> **1** EXACT:
>   (A) precise
>   (B) narrow
>   (C) clean
>   (D) elderly
>   (E) feminine
>
> ● Ⓑ Ⓒ Ⓓ Ⓔ

Se te pedirá que elijas una palabra que significa **lo mismo** que EXACT. EXACT es la palabra de la pregunta.

Prueba de antónimos

Para la prueba de antónimos, las instrucciones son de este tipo:

Decide which word is most nearly the opposite in meaning as the word in capital letters. Fill in the circle containing the letter of your answer.

Las preguntas son como las que se indican a continuación:

> **1** TIDY:
>   (A) limit
>   (B) lost
>   (C) square
>   (D) messy
>   (E) neat
>
> Ⓐ Ⓑ Ⓒ ● Ⓔ

Se te pedirá que elijas una palabra que significa **lo opuesto** a TIDY. TIDY es la palabra de la pregunta.

SUGERENCIA

Si la palabra de la pregunta no te resultara familiar, no te pongas nervioso. Tómate tu tiempo para contestar. Probablemente sepas más de lo que piensas.

Sinónimos y antónimos

Sección de escritura

¿Cómo la respondo?

Paso 1. Lee atentamente las instrucciones. Traza un círculo alrededor de las palabras **same** u **opposite** que figuran en las instrucciones.

Paso 2. Subraya partes que conozcas de la palabra. Tal vez no conozcas una palabra, pero quizá reconozcas una parte de ella. En una palabra como *unheard*, por ejemplo, puedes subrayar el verbo "heard".

Paso 3. Piensa en palabras similares. *Unheard* es como *unlikely, unhappy* y *unbalanced*. ¿Reconoces un patrón que se repite? Estas palabras significan poco probable, descontento o falto de equilibrio. Si piensas que "unheard" significa "not heard", estás en lo cierto.

Paso 4. Piensa en una oración en la cual usar esa palabra. A veces la palabra se usa en una frase común, como por ejemplo, *"That's unheard of."*

Paso 5. Decide si la palabra es positiva o negativa. Las palabras que empiezan con *in-, un-* y *dis-* convierten una palabra en su opuesto.

Paso 6. Descarta las respuestas que creas casi con certeza que están equivocadas. Elige la mejor respuesta y luego indica los motivos de tu elección. Trata de usar tu respuesta en la frase del paso 4 o en otra oración diferente.

> ### SUGERENCIA
> En una **prueba de sinónimos,** una palabra que tenga un significado diferente del de la palabra de la pregunta, es una respuesta equivocada. En una **prueba de antónimos,** una palabra que tenga el mismo significado que el de la palabra de la pregunta es una respuesta equivocada.

Observa el modo en que Hassan, un estudiante, contestó una pregunta de sinónimos:

Decide which word or phrase is most nearly the (same) in meaning as the word in capital letters. Fill in the circle containing the letter of your answer.

Paso 1. En las instrucciones, Hassan trazó un círculo alrededor de la palabra **same.**

Paso 2. Hassan subrayó **dis.** Ya había visto ese prefijo antes en otras palabras.

1 DISREGARD:

- (A) consider
- (B) ignore
- (C) look
- (D) obtain
- (E) read

Paso 6. Hassan recordó que *consider, read, look* y *obtain* eran acciones positivas, de modo que las descartó. Luego, probó su respuesta en la frase que recordó en el paso 4: "ignore the law". Como tenía sentido, eligió la opción **B.**

Paso 3. Hassan recordó que **to diss someone** significa hacerle daño a alguien.

Paso 4. Hassan recordó una frase de la TV: "disregard for the law". Era acerca de gente que no obedecía la ley.

Paso 5. Hassan estaba casi seguro de que la palabra tenía connotaciones negativas.

SPANISH

Sinónimos y antónimos

Pon en práctica tus conocimientos

¡RECUERDA!

√ Traza un círculo alrededor de las palabras **same** u **opposite.**

√ Subraya partes de la palabra que conozcas.

√ Piensa en palabras similares.

√ Piensa en una oración en la cual se usa esa palabra.

√ Decide si la palabra es positiva o negativa.

√ Descarta las respuestas incorrectas.

√ Elige la mejor respuesta y luego úsala en una frase o en una oración

---

Ahora sigue los pasos indicados para contestar las preguntas que figuran a continuación.

Decide which word or phrase is most nearly the same in meaning as the word in capital letters. Fill in the circle containing the letter of your answer.

1 HYPOTHESIS:　　　Ⓐ Ⓑ Ⓒ Ⓓ Ⓔ
  (A) side of a triangle
  (B) theory
  (C) needle
  (D) disease
  (E) report

2 VISAGE:　　　Ⓐ Ⓑ Ⓒ Ⓓ Ⓔ
  (A) foreshadowing
  (B) face
  (C) outlook
  (D) eyesight
  (E) meeting

3 INFATUATED:　　　Ⓐ Ⓑ Ⓒ Ⓓ Ⓔ
  (A) enamored
  (B) overweight
  (C) hinted at
  (D) meaningless
  (E) excited

Decide which word is most nearly the opposite in meaning as the word in capital letters. Fill in the circle containing the letter of your answer.

4 PROPRIETY:　　　Ⓐ Ⓑ Ⓒ Ⓓ Ⓔ
  (A) alive
  (B) rudeness
  (C) ownership
  (D) purchase
  (E) hastiness

5 DISCORD:　　　Ⓐ Ⓑ Ⓒ Ⓓ Ⓔ
  (A) music
  (B) creativity
  (C) doubt
  (D) emptiness
  (E) harmony

SECCIÓN DE LECTURA:
Fíjate en el contexto

Hispanic Immigration in the 1960s   *Sección de lectura*

During the 1960s, the Hispanic population in the United States grew from 3 million to more than 9 million. This increased population came from a number of sources. Spanish-speaking Americans and Hispanics have always been a large and diverse group. America's Hispanic population includes people from many different areas such as Mexico, Puerto Rico, Cuba, the Dominican Republic, Central America, and South America. Because these groups all trace their roots back to Spanish-speaking countries, people often group them together. However, each group has its own history, its own pattern of settlement in the United States, and its own set of economic, social, cultural, and political concerns.

During the 1960s, the number of Mexicans settling in the United States rose. Mexican Americans, who have always been the largest Hispanic group in the United States, once lived mostly in the Southwest and California. Some were the children and grandchildren of the million or so Mexicans who settled in the United States in the decade following Mexico's 1910 revolution. Others came as *braceros,* or seasonal laborers, during the 1940s and 1950s.

Also in the 1960s about a million Puerto Ricans were identified as living in the United States. Most settled in the Northeast, with about 600,000 in New York City alone.

Facing discrimination and lacking needed skills and education, many Puerto Ricans had trouble finding work and getting ahead.

Hundreds of thousands of Cubans fled to the United States after the revolutionary leader Fidel Castro took over in 1959. Most settled in or near Miami, turning it into a boom town. Large Cuban communities also formed in New York City and New Jersey. Many Cubans were academics and professionals, such as doctors and lawyers, who fled to the United States to escape Castro's communist rule.

In addition, tens of thousands of Salvadorans, Guatemalans, Nicaraguans, and Colombians immigrated to the United States after the 1960s to escape civil war and chronic poverty.

Wherever they settled, during the 1960s many Hispanics found ethnic prejudice and discrimination in jobs and housing. Most lived in segregated *barrios,* or Hispanic neighborhoods. The Hispanic jobless rate was higher than that of whites. Many Hispanic families lived in poverty, in contrast to the relative wealth of the rest of the population.

It was time for Hispanics to act. They mobilized to action during the 1960s, 70s, 80s, and 90s, under such dedicated leaders as César Chávez and Dolores Heurta.

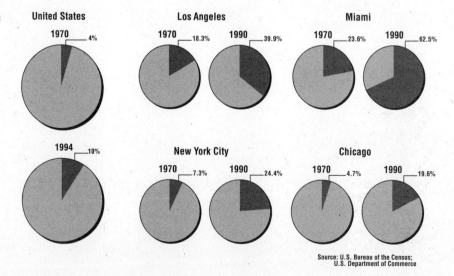

Percentage of Hispanic Population in the United States and Selected Metropolitan Areas, 1970–1994

United States — 1970: 4%; 1994: 10%
Los Angeles — 1970: 18.3%; 1990: 39.9%
Miami — 1970: 23.6%; 1990: 62.5%
New York City — 1970: 7.3%; 1990: 24.4%
Chicago — 1970: 4.7%; 1990: 19.6%

Source: U.S. Bureau of the Census;
U.S. Department of Commerce

Uso de pistas que se hallan en el contexto   *Sección de lectura*

Fíjate en el contexto

A veces quizá no comprendas todas las palabras de un pasaje de lectura. Lo que puedes hacer para deducir qué significa una nueva palabra, es usar **pistas que se hallan en el contexto.**

El **contexto** son las palabras, las oraciones y las ideas que se encuentran antes o después de una palabra o frase.

Cuando leas un pasaje, traza un círculo alrededor de todas las palabras nuevas que no comprendas. Luego, busca pistas en el contexto; éstas son las palabras o frases que sugieren el significado de una nueva palabra. Analiza las palabras rodeadas por un círculo y las pistas que sugieren, dentro del contexto, cuál es el significado de dichas palabras:

Tipo de pista	Significado	Ejemplo
Sinónimos	Palabra que significa lo mismo que la palabra nueva.	"ethnic prejudice and discrimination"
Antónimos	Palabra que significa lo opuesto a la palabra nueva.	"live in poverty, in contrast to the relative wealth of the rest of the population"
Definición	Expresar la palabra nueva mediante la explicación de su significado.	"came as braceros, or seasonal laborers"
Descripción	Decir algo más acerca de la palabra nueva.	"the revolutionary leader Fidel Castro took over in 1959. . . escaping Castro's communist rule."
Ejemplo	Dar un ejemplo en el que se utilice la palabra nueva.	"Many Cubans were academics and professionals such as doctors and lawyers."

> ### SUGERENCIA
> Recuerda, no es imprescindible que entiendas todas y cada una de las palabras de una lectura. Traza un círculo solamente alrededor de las palabras nuevas que son clave para comprender el pasaje.

Uso de pistas que se hallan en el contexto   *Sección de lectura*

Fíjate en el contexto

Para usar las pistas del contexto, haz lo siguiente:

Paso 1. Traza un círculo alrededor de la palabra o frase que no comprendes.

Paso 2. Subraya las frases y las ideas clave de la oración. Busca palabras que sugieran sinónimos, antónimos, ejemplos, etc.

Paso 3. Expresa la idea principal del párrafo en el que se encuentra la palabra nueva.

Paso 4. Di la oración con tus propias palabras.

Paso 5. Adivina el significado de la palabra nueva. Utiliza lo que subrayaste para demostrar que tu elección fue la correcta.

Para comprender la palabra *segregated* en "Hispanic... ," el estudiante Kazuyo hizo lo siguiente:

Paso 1. Traza un círculo alrededor de la palabra que no comprendes.	Wherever they settled, during the 1960s many Hispanics found ethnic prejudice and discrimination in jobs and housing. Most lived in (segregated) *barrios,* or Hispanic neighborhoods. The Hispanic jobless rate was higher than that of whites. Many Hispanic families lived in poverty, in contrast to the relative wealth of the rest of the population. It was time for Hispanics to act. They mobilized to action during the 1960s, 70s, 80s, and 90s, under such dedicated leaders as César Chávez and Dolores Huerta.	Paso 4. Kayzo dijo que el párrafo era acerca de que los hispanos vivían en barrios diferentes o separados.
Paso 2. Subraya las frases y las ideas clave de la oración que está antes y después.		Paso 5. Kayzo adivinó que *segregated* significa "different" o "separated."
Paso 3. Kayzo dijo que el párrafo se refería a que los hispanos eran pobres.		

Pon en práctica tus conocimientos

A. Las siguientes palabras y frases son del pasaje "Hispanic Immigration...". Traza un círculo alrededor de ellas y sigue las indicaciones de los pasos 1 a 5 antes mencionadas, para adivinar su significado. En los espacios en blanco, escribe lo que creas que es correcto.

Creo que el significado es:

1. diverse _____

2. pattern of settlement _____

3. lacking _____

4. mobilized _____

SPANISH

Uso de conocimientos previos

Sección de lectura

Fíjate en el contexto

Algunos pasajes podrían referirse a algo sobre lo cual no conoces mucho. Pero siempre sabrás algo acerca del tema. Podrás utilizar tus **conocimientos previos,** es decir, lo que ya sabes sobre algo en particular para comprender el tema tratado en el pasaje.

Antes de leer

Antes de leer el pasaje, tienes que formarte una idea acerca del tema. Haz lo siguiente:

Paso 1. Traza un círculo alrededor del título del pasaje.

Paso 2. Traza un círculo alrededor de los títulos de las tablas o gráficas que pueda haber.

Paso 3. Redacta el tema con tus propias palabras.

Paso 4. Escribe tres o cuatro cosas que ya sepas acerca del tema.

Antes de leer el pasaje, observa cómo la estudiante Lisa siguió estos pasos:

| Paso 1. Traza un círculo alrededor del título. |
| Paso 2. Traza un círculo alrededor de los títulos de las tablas o gráficas que pueda haber. |

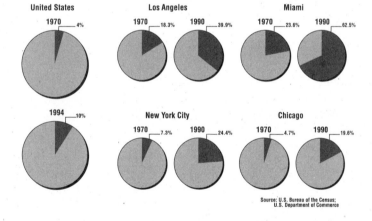

Hispanic Immigration in the 1960s

Source: U.S. Bureau of the Census; U.S. Department of Commerce

Lisa redactó el tema de acuerdo a lo que había entendido: Mexicanos que viven en distintas ciudades de los Estados Unidos.

Paso 4. Lisa escribió tres cosas que ya sabía acerca del tema:
1. Algunos Mexicanos han venido a los Estados Unidos.
2. Algunos Mexicanos viven en California porque es cerca de México.
3. Hay muchos Cubanos que se van a vivir a Miami.

A. Lee los títulos del pasaje que figuran a continuación. Escribe dos cosas que ya sepas acerca de cada uno.

1. Up in Smoke: Cigarette Smoking

_____

2. Year-Round Schooling: A Good Idea

_____

3. Training Cats and Dogs

SPANISH

Uso de conocimientos previos

Sección de lectura

Fíjate en el contexto

A medida que vayas leyendo

A medida que vayas leyendo el pasaje, probablemente verás palabras nuevas que no entenderás. Puedes utilizar los conocimientos que tengas para comprender de qué se trata el pasaje. Sigue estos pasos:

Paso 1. A medida que leas, traza un círculo alrededor de cualquier palabra nueva que no entiendas.

Paso 2. Observa las palabras que marcaste con un círculo. Determina cuáles son importantes y cuáles realmente no necesitas saber.

Paso 3. Lee la oración que está antes y la que está después de la palabra nueva. Escribe dos cosas que conozcas acerca del tema.

Paso 4. Trata de adivinar qué significa la palabra nueva. Describe dos razones que respalden tu elección.

Observa el modo en que Lisa realizó los pasos del 1 al 4 para comprender las palabras desconocidas del pasaje "Hispanic Immigration in the 1960s."

Paso 1. A medida que Lisa leía, trazaba un círculo alrededor de las palabras que no conocía.

> Wherever they settled, during the 1960s many Hispanics found (ethnic) prejudice and discrimination in jobs and housing. Most lived in (segregated) *barrios*, or Hispanic neighborhoods. The Hispanic jobless rate was nearly 50 percent higher than that of whites. Many Hispanic families lived in poverty.

Paso 4. Lisa supuso que "ethnic" tenía que ver con algo relacionado con un grupo racial en particular, como el hispano.

Paso 2. Lisa no conocía el significado de "segregated," pero sabía lo que era un *barrio*. Decidió determinar el significado de "ethnic."

Paso 3. Lisa escribió dos cosas que sabía acerca de la discriminación y de los barrios hispanos:
1. "Prejuicio" tiene que ver con gente a la que no le gustan los hispanos.
2. No hay muchos blancos que vivan en *barrios*.

SUGERENCIA
Si entiendes la idea principal de una oración sin conocer una palabra, simplemente saltea la palabra y continúa leyendo.

A. Las siguientes palabras son del pasaje "Hispanic Immigration…"
Utiliza tus conocimientos previos para determinar su significado. En el espacio en blanco próximo a cada palabra, escribe lo que sepas acerca de ella.

	Creo que el significado es:	**Lo que ya sé acerca del tema es:**
1. segregated	_____	_____
2. revolutionary	_____	_____
3. trace their roots	_____	_____

SPANISH

SECCION DE LECTURA:
¿Cuál es la pregunta y cómo la contesto?

Writing by Moonlight

Murasaki Shikibu was an outstanding student, but her father was not proud of her. Instead, he wished she were a boy. In tenth-century Japan, girls were neither valued nor expected to excel in school.

However, Murasaki knew, for example, how to write and read in Chinese, even though many people thought women were not smart enough to learn such skills. Murasaki often had to hide her knowledge from others because she feared she would be rejected.

Despite her father's and society's disapproval, Murasaki was determined to be a writer. She liked to gaze at the moon and scribble by its light because no one bothered her at that time. People believed that women should not look at the moon because it allegedly caused them to age, and old women were not treated well. Murasaki did not care. She began referring to herself as a disgusting old fossil and kept staring at the moon. She was writing notes for a novel.

Fortunately, Murasaki's father found her a job as a lady-in-waiting, or servant, to the teenage empress. Murasaki had more time to write because the job was not demanding.

She disliked working at the palace, though, because people were occupied with gossip, bad poetry, and other shallow pursuits. Women and men were separated, and if a man entered a room, a woman had to go behind a screen. Everyone in the palace mocked Murasaki's work on her novel.

She continued to write, struggling with a lack of basic supplies such as ink and paper (the latter was rare in tenth-century Japan). The empress, who had heard that Murasaki knew Chinese, eventually solved that problem. She engaged Murasaki to teach her Chinese, even though society disapproved. In gratitude the empress gave Murasaki paper, ink, and brushes for writing.

Murasaki simplified her life so that she could devote most of her attention and energy to writing. She avoided social life in the palace, even during cold winters. She warmed her room by setting charcoal on fire in a hibachi. Her primary food was plain and dry rice cakes. Murasaki's only entertainment was playing gloomy music on a string instrument called a *koto*. Not surprisingly, she considered becoming a nun in the Buddhist faith.

Murasaki's devotion to writing paid off, although her accomplishments were not recognized for centuries. Many contemporary scholars believe that she wrote the first and oldest novel in human history—*The Tale of Genji*. Murasaki's novel revolutionized literature. She wrote about nature, people's feelings, and other topics in completely original ways. Some of her writing techniques were so advanced that they were not used again in literature for hundreds of years.

Ironically, despite her achievement, we do not know Murasaki's real name and never will. At that time, the names of Japanese women were not considered to be important. The name we know this author by today is a combination of her father's title and the name of the heroine of her famous novel.

Cómo encontrar datos de respaldo   *Sección de lectura*

¿Cuál es la pregunta?

En algunas preguntas se te pide que elijas una respuesta basada en hechos o evidencias aportadas por la lectura. A menudo las preguntas son del siguiente tipo:

1 The passage provides evidence that Murasaki is—

    A determined

    B lazy

    C outgoing

    D confused

En primer lugar, asegúrate de que entiendes las palabras de la pregunta. Estas palabras podrían ser de utilidad:

provides evidence	*presenta hechos, pistas*
sufficient	*suficiente*
suggests that	*sugiere que*
shows how	*prueban*
reveals	*te indican cómo*

Tales preguntas te piden que elijas una respuesta que puedas demostrar que es cierta. Deberás elegir una respuesta sólo cuando puedas encontrar una evidencia en el pasaje que pruebe que tu elección es la correcta.

> **SUGERENCIA**
> Cuando tomes la prueba, intenta expresar la pregunta del siguiente modo:
> **En la lectura se dice que…**

A. Vuelve a escribir cada una de las siguientes preguntas. La primera te la damos hecha.

1. The passage provides evidence that Murasaki is—

   The reading says that Murasaki is _____

2. The writer suggests that Murasaki—

_____

3. The words show how Murasaki—

_____

SPANISH

Cómo encontrar datos de respaldo

Sección de lectura

¿Cómo la contesto?

Paso 1. Analiza las respuestas. Descarta dos que creas casi con certeza que están equivocadas.

Paso 2. Regresa a la lectura. Busca palabras o frases en las respuestas.

Paso 3. Subraya las frases de la lectura que demuestren que una respuesta es correcta.

Paso 4. Elige la respuesta que creas que es correcta.

Paso 5. Vuelve a leer lo que subrayaste en la lectura. ¿Con eso pruebas que tu elección fue la correcta?

> ### SUGERENCIA
> Recuerda que las evidencias y las pistas podrían insinuar un enunciado, no decirlo exactamente.

Mira el modelo que figura a continuación. Observa cómo la estudiante Sara cumplió con los pasos del 1 al 5 para contestar una pregunta acerca del pasaje "Writing by Moonlight."

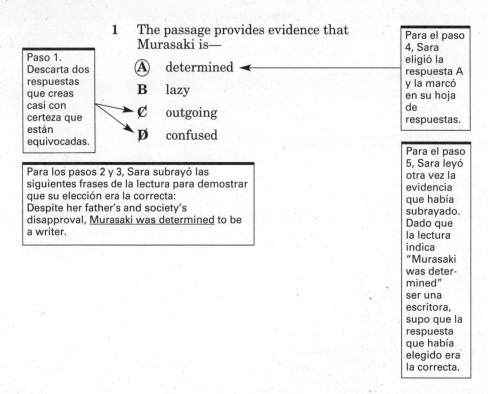

1   The passage provides evidence that Murasaki is—

A   determined

B   lazy

C   outgoing

D   confused

Paso 1. Descarta dos respuestas que creas casi con certeza que están equivocadas.

Para los pasos 2 y 3, Sara subrayó las siguientes frases de la lectura para demostrar que su elección era la correcta:
Despite her father's and society's disapproval, Murasaki was determined to be a writer.

Para el paso 4, Sara eligió la respuesta A y la marcó en su hoja de respuestas.

Para el paso 5, Sara leyó otra vez la evidencia que había subrayado. Dado que la lectura indica "Murasaki was determined" ser una escritora, supo que la respuesta que había elegido era la correcta.

SPANISH

Cómo encontrar datos de respaldo

Sección de lectura

Pon en práctica tus conocimientos

¡RECUERDA!

√ Descarta dos respuestas.

√ Busca palabras en las respuestas de la lectura.

√ Subraya los datos de respaldo que haya en la lectura.

√ Elige la respuesta.

√ Explica tu respuesta.

Las siguientes preguntas se refieren al pasaje "Writing by Moonlight". Lee las respuestas y elige una. Copia la evidencia de la lectura en los espacios a continuación de cada pregunta.

1 The passage reveals that—

A Murasaki disliked being a student

B girls were not valued as students in tenth-century Japan

C girls were not valued as servants in tenth-century Japan

D the empress had many servants

Evidencia

_____

_____

_____

_____

2 Murasaki shows that she does not enjoy the palace by—

F writing notes for a novel

G attending school

H gazing at the moon

J passing time in her room

Evidencia

_____

_____

_____

_____

3 The passage provides sufficient evidence to show that Murasaki—

A should not have learned Chinese

B deserves recognition for her accomplishments

C did not like living simply

D should not have looked at the moon

Evidencia

_____

_____

_____

_____

SPANISH

Determinación del objetivo

Sección de lectura

¿Cuál es la pregunta?

En algunas preguntas se te pide que identifiques el punto principal de un pasaje. Es decir, se te pide que **determines el objetivo.** Las preguntas son como las que se indican a continuación:

1. The author's main point is to—

2. The author's purpose in writing this passage is to—

3. The main purpose of the paragraph is to—

4. What is the point of this essay?

En primer lugar, recuerda que debes comprender las palabras de la pregunta. Las siguientes palabras podrían ser de utilidad:

main point	*idea central, intención*
purpose	*más importante, finalidad*
in order to	*para que él /ella pueda*

En estas preguntas se te pide que decidas para qué se escribió la lectura (o parte de ella). Deberás elegir una respuesta que explique las razones que llevaron al escritor a escribir el pasaje analizado.

SUGERENCIA

Recuerda marcar la parte del pasaje a la que se refiere la pregunta. He aquí algunas pistas:

initial, opening paragraph   *primer párrafo*
final, closing paragraph   *último párrafo*

A. Traza un círculo alrededor de la parte de la lectura acerca de la cual se formula la pregunta. Luego traza un círculo alrededor de la frase que se refiere a esto. Subraya las palabras *purpose, reason* o *main point* de la pregunta. La primera pregunta ya está hecha.

Paragraph

1. The author's <u>purpose</u> in writing the (opening paragraph)—   ① 2 3 4 5 6 7 8 9 10

2. The main point of the second sentence of the closing paragraph is to—   1 2 3 4 5 6 7 8 9 10

3. This essay is saying that—   1 2 3 4 5 6 7 8 9 10

4. The main purpose of the final paragraph is to—   1 2 3 4 5 6 7 8 9 10

5. The author wrote the initial paragraph in order to—   1 2 3 4 5 6 7 8 9 10

Determinación del objetivo

Sección de lectura

¿Cómo la contesto?

Paso 1. Lee la pregunta. Traza un círculo alrededor de la parte de la lectura a la que se refiere la pregunta. Subraya palabras tales como *reason, purpose* o *main point.*

Paso 2. Analiza las respuestas. Descarta las dos que creas casi con certeza que están equivocadas.

Paso 3. Regresa a la sección destacada con un círculo. Busca cuál es el punto central.

Paso 4. Subraya las frases que describen a la persona o al punto central y/o el modo en que actúa.

Paso 5. Lee atentamente todas las respuestas. Elige la que te parezca correcta.

Paso 6. Lee lo que subrayaste. ¿Prueba que tu respuesta es la correcta?

Mira el modelo que figura a continuación. Observa cómo el estudiante Jamal cumplió con los pasos del 1 al 6 para contestar una pregunta acerca de una parte de "Writing by Moonlight."

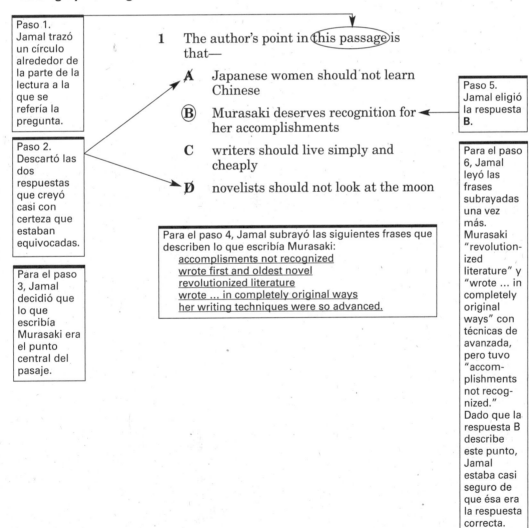

Paso 1.
Jamal trazó un círculo alrededor de la parte de la lectura a la que se refería la pregunta.

Paso 2.
Descartó las dos respuestas que creyó casi con certeza que estaban equivocadas.

Para el paso 3, Jamal decidió que lo que escribía Murasaki era el punto central del pasaje.

1   The author's point in this passage is that—

A   Japanese women should not learn Chinese

B   Murasaki deserves recognition for her accomplishments

C   writers should live simply and cheaply

D   novelists should not look at the moon

Para el paso 4, Jamal subrayó las siguientes frases que describen lo que escribía Murasaki:
    accomplisments not recognized
    wrote first and oldest novel
    revolutionized literature
    wrote ... in completely original ways
    her writing techniques were so advanced.

Paso 5.
Jamal eligió la respuesta B.

Para el paso 6, Jamal leyó las frases subrayadas una vez más. Murasaki "revolutionized literature" y "wrote ... in completely original ways" con técnicas de avanzada, pero tuvo "accomplishments not recognized." Dado que la respuesta B describe este punto, Jamal estaba casi seguro de que ésa era la respuesta correcta.

SPANISH

NAME_____ Date _____

Determinación del objetivo

Sección de lectura

Pon en práctica tus conocimientos

> **¡RECUERDA!**
>
> √ Subraya palabras tales como reason y purpose en la pregunta. Traza un círculo alrededor de la parte de la lectura a la que se refiere la pregunta.
>
> √ Descarta las dos respuestas que creas casi con certeza que están equivocadas.
>
> √ Busca el punto principal y subraya las frases que se refieren a él.
>
> √ Elige la respuesta que te parezca correcta.
>
> √ Utiliza lo que subrayaste para demostrar que tu respuesta es la correcta.

Las siguientes preguntas se refieren al pasaje "Writing by Moonlight". Léelas y elige una respuesta. En los espacios siguientes a cada pregunta, copia lo que subrayaste en la lectura para justificar tu respuesta.

1   The author wrote Paragraph 3 in order to—

   A   show that Murasaki persisted in spite of much disapproval.

   B   describe the beliefs of tenth-century Japan.

   C   show how Murasaki was acting foolishly.

   D   warn people about looking at the moon.

INFORMACIÓN DESCRIPTIVA:

_____

_____

_____

_____

2   The purpose of describing Murasaki's life in Paragraph 7 is to—

   F   describe typical palace life.

   G   show that Murasaki was a poor servant.

   H   show her dedication to writing through difficult conditions.

   J   describe Murasaki's entertainment.

INFORMACIÓN DESCRIPTIVA:

_____

_____

_____

_____

3   With this essay, the author is making the point that—

   A   Murasaki did not like cold winters, gossip, or joyful music.

   B   it is foolish to stare at the moon.

   C   women were not treated well in tenth-century Japan.

   D   despite opposition, Murasaki wrote what was probably the first novel.

INFORMACIÓN DESCRIPTIVA:

_____

_____

_____

_____

The Aztecs Control Central Mexico   *Sección de lectura*

Aztecs Build an Empire

The Aztecs arrived in the Valley of Mexico around A.D. 1299. It was the home of several small cities that had survived the end of Toltec rule. The Aztecs, who were then called the Mexica, were a poor, nomadic people. Fierce and ambitious, the Aztecs soon adapted to local ways. They found paid work as soldiers for local rulers.

According to an Aztec legend, the Aztecs' sun god, Huitzilopochtli (wee-tsee-loh-POHCH-tlee), told them to start a city of their own. He said to look for a place where an eagle stood on a cactus, holding a snake in its mouth. Part of the legend is told with these words:

> The place where the eagle screams,
> where he spreads his wings;
> the place where he feeds,
> where the fish jump,
> where the serpents
> coil up and hiss!
> This shall be Mexico Tenochtitlán
> and many things shall happen!
> —Cronica Mexicayotl

The Aztecs found this place on a small island in Lake Texcoco, at the center of the valley. There, in 1324, they started their city and named it Tenochtitlán (teh-NOCH-tee-TLAHN).

Aztecs Grow Stronger

In 1428, the Aztecs joined with two other cities—Texcoco and Tlacopán—to form the Triple Alliance. This group of cities became the leading power in the Valley of Mexico. The Triple Alliance soon gained control over neighboring regions. By the early 1500s, the alliance controlled the huge area that stretched from central Mexico to the Atlantic and Pacific coasts and south into Oaxaca. Their empire was divided into 38 provinces, or states. It had an estimated population of between 5 and 15 million people.

The Aztec state was powerful because of its military rule and its wealth from the taxes paid by the people it conquered. The Aztecs loosely controlled most of their empire. They often let local leaders rule their own regions. The Aztecs did demand tribute, however, of gold, corn, cocoa, cotton, jade and other products. If local rulers refused to pay tribute, the Aztec warriors responded brutally. They destroyed villages and captured or killed the people.

Problems in the Aztec Empire

Eventually, the Aztecs' huge empire caused problems for them. In 1502 a new ruler, Montezuma II, became emperor. Under Montezuma, the Aztec empire began to weaken. For nearly a century, the Aztecs had been demanding tribute and sacrifices from the provinces. Now, with the population of Tenochtitlán growing, the emperor demanded even more tribute and sacrifices. Some provinces revolted. The people were unhappy with the cruel and demanding Aztecs. These revolts were the beginning of a period of instability and unrest. During this time, the Aztec military was often sent to the provinces to stop rebellions.

Montezuma tried to reduce pressure on the provinces. He reduced the number of government officials. Still, the people in the provinces were unhappy and resentful. Then, in addition to the problems at home, another threat appeared: the arrival of the Spanish.

SPANISH

Cómo efectuar inferencias

Sección de lectura

¿Cuál es la pregunta?

En algunas preguntas se te pide que **realices una inferencia** basándote en la lectura. Las preguntas son como las que se indican a continuación:

1. From this passage, you can infer—
2. According to the author, one has reason to believe—
3. The second paragraph suggests that—
4. Based on the information, one can tell that—
5. Information in the passage suggests that—
6. What probably made the Azetecs good warriors was—

En primer lugar, asegúrate de comprender las palabras de la pregunta. Las siguientes palabras podrían ser de utilidad:

infer	*suponer, adivinar*
gives (one) reason to believe	*hace pensar que*
suggest	*da pistas acerca de, sugiere*
(you) can tell that	*hay pruebas que demuestran que*
probably	*probablemente*

Mediante estas preguntas se te pide que infieras algo basándote en las pistas que se mencionan en el pasaje. Deberás elegir una respuesta que puedas deducir de las frases de la lectura

> **SUGERENCIA**
> En la lectura no encontrarás la respuesta exacta. Trata de deducir la mejor respuesta basándote en dos o tres pistas que figuren en la lectura.

A. Subraya la palabra o frase que te indique que **debes inferir algo** en las preguntas que figuran a continuación. Luego traza un círculo alrededor del punto principal de la pregunta. La primera pregunta ya está hecha.

1. The fact that the Aztecs found paid work as soldiers suggests that—
2. The alliance with Texcoco and Tlacopán gives one reason to believe—
3. From Montezuma's actions you can tell that—
4. From the empire's wealth, you can infer that—
5. According to the author, one can tell that—

Cómo efectuar inferencias

Sección de lectura

¿Cómo la contesto?

Paso 1. Subraya las palabras o frases de la pregunta en que se te pide que efectúes una inferencia. Traza un círculo alrededor de lo que se solicita en la pregunta.

Paso 2. Lee las respuestas con atención. Descarta dos respuestas que creas casi con certeza que están equivocadas.

Paso 3. Vuelve a leer el texto. Subraya las frases que se refieren al tema o punto principal.

Paso 4. Lee las respuestas. Luego lee las frases que hayas subrayado. Elige la que concuerde más con la información de la lectura.

Paso 5. Lee lo que subrayaste en el texto. ¿Respalda esto la respuesta que elegiste?

Mira el modelo que figura a continuación. Observa cómo Li cumplió con los pasos del 1 al 5 para contestar una pregunta del pasaje "The Aztecs Control Central Mexico."

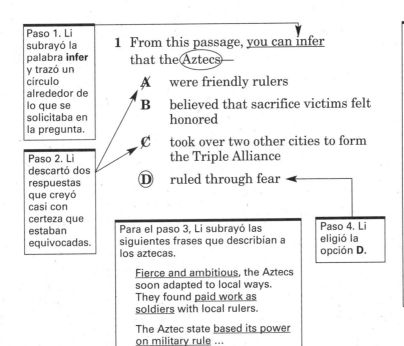

Paso 1. Li subrayó la palabra **infer** y trazó un círculo alrededor de lo que se solicitaba en la pregunta.

Paso 2. Li descartó dos respuestas que creyó casi con certeza que estaban equivocadas.

1 From this passage, <u>you can infer</u> that the (Aztecs)—

   A   were friendly rulers

   B   believed that sacrifice victims felt honored

   C   took over two other cities to form the Triple Alliance

   D   ruled through fear

Para el paso 3, Li subrayó las siguientes frases que describían a los aztecas.

<u>Fierce and ambitious</u>, the Aztecs soon adapted to local ways. They found <u>paid work as soldiers</u> with local rulers.

The Aztec state <u>based its power on military rule</u> ...

... the Aztec <u>warriors responded brutally</u>.

Paso 4. Li eligió la opción **D**.

Para el paso 5, Li leyó otra vez las frases subrayadas. Los aztecas eran "fierce and ambitious," trabajaban "as soldiers," utilizaban "military rule" y "responded brutally." Dado que esto describía a un pueblo que infundía temor en otros pueblos, Li estuvo casi segura de que la respuesta correcta era **D**.

SPANISH

Cómo efectuar inferencias

Sección de lectura

Pon en práctica tus conocimientos

Las siguientes preguntas se refieren al pasaje "The Aztecs Control Central Mexico". Léelas todas y elige una respuesta. Escribe el punto principal de cada pregunta y copia las pistas que hayas encontrado en la lectura que apoyen tu respuesta.

1 The fact that Aztecs worked as paid soldiers suggests that they—

    A learned military skills before forming an empire

    B needed to protect their way of life

    C did not like their current home

    D were ready to move to a new valley

Tema/Pistas:

_____

_____

_____

_____

2 The alliance with Texcoco and Tlacopán gives one reason to believe—

    F these two cities were weak

    G the Aztecs were weaker than these two cities

    H the Aztecs did not war with all their neighbors

    J the Aztecs enjoyed life as nomads

Tema/Pistas:

_____

_____

_____

3 From Montezuma's actions you can tell that—

    A the Aztecs were becoming more religious

    B the population enjoyed being part of a large empire

    C he had weak control of his empire

    D he did not want to be emperor

Tema/Pistas:

_____

_____

_____

_____

Cómo efectuar predicciones

Sección de lectura

¿Cuál es la pregunta?

En algunas preguntas se te pide que elijas una respuesta basándote en lo que piensas que podría ocurrir más adelante. Es decir, en estas preguntas se te pide que **efectúes predicciones.** Los siguientes son ejemplos de frases en las que se te pide que realices predicciones.

1. The Aztecs' empire will most likely—

2. You can tell from the passage that the Spanish will probably—

3. What is Montezuma likely to do next?

4. Judging by the passage, which action will the Spaniards most likely take?

5. Which of the following is least likely to happen?

En primer lugar, asegúrate de que entiendes las palabras de la pregunta. Las frases que siguen pueden usarse en preguntas donde se te pide que hagas predicciones. Observa su significado.

most likely	*probablemente*
least likely	*probablemente no*
you can tell	*puedes deducir que*

En estas preguntas se te pide que adivines lo que hará una persona o lo que ocurrirá más adelante. Deberás elegir una respuesta basándote en lo que ya ha sucedido según el pasaje.

Lee atentamente la pregunta. Estos son los pasos a seguir:

1. Subraya el sujeto principal, es decir, la persona o cosa sobre la que harás la predicción.

2. Si la pregunta hiciera referencia a un tiempo determinado (this evening, in the future, next) traza un círculo alrededor de ella.

3. Si la pregunta contuviera las palabras least o not, subráyalas con una línea doble.

Observa cómo la estudiante María resolvió la pregunta que figura a continuación.

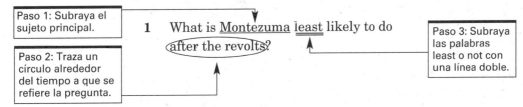

A. Lee atentamente las siguientes preguntas. Subraya el sujeto. Si se hiciera referencia a un tiempo en particular, traza un círculo a su alrededor. Si la pregunta contuviera las palabras *least* o *not*, subráyalas con una línea doble.

1. In the future the Aztecs' empire will most likely—

2. You can tell from the passage that the Spanish will probably not—

3. What will Montezuma be least likely to do next?

4. Which of the following is likely to happen after the Spanish arrive?

Cómo efectuar predicciones

Sección de lectura

¿Cómo la contesto?

Paso 1. Lee la pregunta. Subraya el sujeto principal. Si la pregunta se refiriera a un tiempo determinado, traza un círculo a su alrededor. Si la pregunta contuviera las palabras *least* o *not,* subráyalas con una línea doble.

Paso 2. Analiza las respuestas con atención. Descarta las dos respuestas que creas casi con certeza que están equivocadas.

Paso 3. Vuelve a leer el texto. Subraya las pistas referentes a los sentimientos o acciones vinculados al sujeto.

Paso 4. Subraya lo que ya sucedió.

Paso 5. Lee detenidamente las respuestas posibles. Elige la que te parezca mejor.

Paso 6. Vuelve a leer las pistas que has subrayado. ¿Respaldan éstas la respuesta que elegiste? Vuelve a leer tu respuesta.

Mira el modelo que figura a continuación. Observa cómo María cumplió con los pasos del 1 al 6 para contestar una pregunta del pasaje "The Aztecs Control Central Mexico."

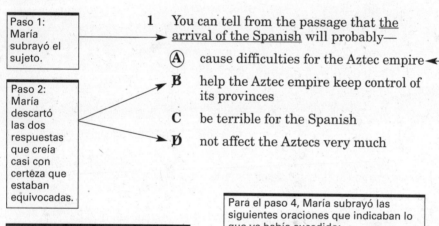

Paso 1:
María subrayó el sujeto.

1   You can tell from the passage that the arrival of the Spanish will probably—

   (A)   cause difficulties for the Aztec empire

   B   help the Aztec empire keep control of its provinces

   C   be terrible for the Spanish

   D   not affect the Aztecs very much

Paso 5.
María eligió la respuesta A.

Paso 2:
María descartó las dos respuestas que creía casi con certeza que estaban equivocadas.

Para el paso 6, María volvió a leer las oraciones. Los españoles fueron una amenaza. Por lo tanto, María estuvo casi segura de que el imperio azteca no iba más que a empeorar. La respuesta **A** es la correcta.

En el paso 3, María subrayó las siguientes palabras del pasaje, las cuales aportaban información acerca del sujeto: ...

... another threat appeared: the arrival of the Spanish.

Para el paso 4, María subrayó las siguientes oraciones que indicaban lo que ya había sucedido:

... the Aztecs' huge empire caused problems for them.

Under Montezuma, the Aztec empire began to weaken.

... revolts were the beginning of a period of instability and unrest.

SUGERENCIA

Cuando taches las respuestas, sólo tacha la letra. Luego de haber seguido todos los pasos, tal vez decidas que una de estas respuestas es correcta después de todo.

Cómo efectuar predicciones

Sección de lectura

Pon en práctica tus conocimientos

¡RECUERDA!

√ Lee la pregunta. Subraya el sujeto. Traza un círculo alrededor de la referencia de tiempo. Si la pregunta contuviera las palabras *least* o *not*, subráyalas con una línea doble.

√ Descarta las dos preguntas que creas casi con certeza que están equivocadas.

√ En el texto, subraya las pistas referentes al sujeto.

√ Subraya lo que ya sucedió.

√ Elige una respuesta.

√ Compara tu respuesta al contenido de la lectura.

Las siguientes preguntas se refieren al pasaje "The Aztecs Control Central Mexico". Léelas y elige tus respuestas. En el espacio próximo a cada pregunta, copia lo que encontraste en la lectura que respalde la elección de tu respuesta.

Pistas:

1   The Spanish will probably not—

    A   help Montezuma with the empire   _____

    B   conquer the Aztecs   _____

    C   contribute to Montezuma's difficulties   _____

    D   battle the Aztecs   _____

Pistas:

2   What will Montezuma be least likely to do next?

    F   look for ways to stop revolts   _____

    G   maintain the number of officials   _____

    H   resist Spanish influence   _____

    J   welcome the support of the Spanish   _____

Pistas:

3   After the Spanish arrive, the Aztecs' empire will most likely—

    A   remain the same   _____

    B   continue to do poorly   _____

    C   increase its wealth   _____

    D   celebrate   _____

SPANISH

Built for Speed

Sección de lectura

According to some scientists, the enormous dinosaur *Tyrannosaurus rex* could run as fast as 34 miles per hour (mph). This huge creature could achieve such high speeds because it had unusually large thigh muscles.

However, a *Tyrannosaurus rex* could not move as quickly as a modern-day whippet (a type of dog), horse, or cheetah. All of those animals can run at speeds of more than 40 mph. Human beings, although they did not exist while dinosaurs were alive, would have been comparatively slow and easy prey for a *Tyrannosaurus rex*. A person's maximum speed is 23 mph.

Biped mammals, those that walk and run on two legs, include human beings. People cannot achieve the high speeds of quadrupeds—animals that walk and run on four legs—because two of their limbs, the arms, are hanging uselessly at their sides.

Horses are quadrupeds that can use all four limbs when running, which enables a maximum speed almost twice as fast as that of human beings. When horses run, they never have more than two hooves touching the ground. Horses have no ground contact at all for about a quarter of the time they run. This enables them to achieve a maximum speed of 43 mph.

Whippets and cheetahs stay off the ground even longer while they run—they are airborne for about twice the time that a cantering horse is. Cheetahs, the speediest mammals on the planet, have hip joints and shoulder blades that move easily. In addition, they have very flexible skeletons that allow their backbones to ripple up and down during a run. These features give cheetahs the ability to lengthen their stride—to about twice that of a horse—and move their legs very fast.

This ability to attain a high running speed is not as useful as it might seem. Humans and horses cannot run as fast as cheetahs, but they have good endurance. Cheetahs have such poor endurance that they can only keep up their maximum speed for about 15 seconds. Consequently, if a slow but determined *Tyrannosaurus rex* had encountered a modern-day cheetah, that dinosaur could have caught the fastest mammal on Earth.

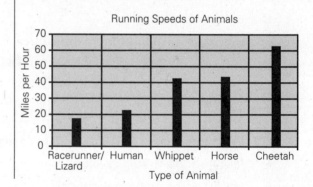

Running Speeds of Animals

Elección de la idea principal

Sección de lectura

¿Cuál es la pregunta?

En algunas preguntas se te pedirá que elijas la idea principal del texto. La idea principal es el punto clave de un párrafo o de un pasaje. A menudo, las preguntas son como las que se indican a continuación:

1. The passage evaluates—

2. Which statement best expresses the main idea in Paragraph 5?

3. According to the passage, speed—

4. The main idea of the final paragraph—

En primer lugar, asegúrate de que entiendes las palabras de la pregunta. Deberás conocer las siguientes palabras y frases:

evaluates	*compara, dice*
expresses	*expresa, se refiere a*
according to	*a causa de lo que dice*

En estas preguntas se te pide que decidas cuál es la idea principal del pasaje. Deberás elegir una respuesta que se refiera a todas las ideas mencionadas en el pasaje.

Lee atentamente la pregunta y sigue estos pasos:

1. Subraya las palabras *evaluate, express, according to* o *main idea.*

2. Si la pregunta tuviera un sujeto, subráyalo con una línea doble.

3. En la pregunta, traza un círculo alrededor de la parte de la lectura a la cual hace referencia la pregunta.

Observa como el estudiante Winston siguió los siguientes pasos:

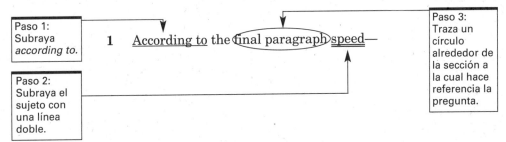

A. Lee atentamente las siguientes preguntas. Subraya las palabras *evaluate, express* y *according to.* Subraya el sujeto con una línea doble. Traza un círculo alrededor de la parte de la lectura a la cual hace referencia la pregunta.

1. The first paragraph evaluates—

2. Which statement best expresses the main idea in Paragraph 5?

3. According to the third paragraph, biped mammals—

4. The main idea of the final paragraph—

Elección de la idea principal

Sección de lectura

¿Cómo la contesto?

Paso 1. Lee la pregunta. Subraya las palabras evaluate, express, according to o main idea. Subraya el sujeto con doble raya.

Paso 2. Traza un círculo alrededor de la parte de la lectura a la cual hace referencia la pregunta.

Paso 3. Descarta las respuestas falsas o que no se mencionan en la lectura.

Paso 4. Lee atentamente las respuestas. Elige la respuesta que creas correcta.

Paso 5. Vuelve a leer el pasaje. Subraya una oración de cada párrafo que respalde tu elección de respuesta. Si el pasaje fuera de un solo párrafo, subraya el sujeto y el verbo de cada una de las oraciones que lo componen.

Paso 6. Vuelve a leer lo que subrayaste. Explica por qué eso respalda tu elección.

Mira el modelo que figura a continuación. Observa cómo Winston cumplió con los pasos del 1 al 6 para contestar una pregunta del pasaje "Built for Speed."

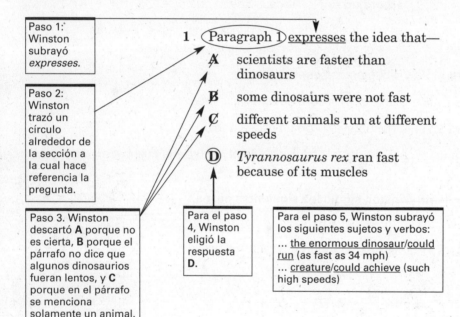

Paso 1: Winston subrayó *expresses*.

Paso 2: Winston trazó un círculo alrededor de la sección a la cual hace referencia la pregunta.

Paso 3. Winston descartó **A** porque no es cierta, **B** porque el párrafo no dice que algunos dinosaurios fueran lentos, y **C** porque en el párrafo se menciona solamente un animal.

1 Paragraph 1 expresses the idea that—

A scientists are faster than dinosaurs

B some dinosaurs were not fast

C different animals run at different speeds

D *Tyrannosaurus rex* ran fast because of its muscles

Para el paso 4, Winston eligió la respuesta **D**.

Para el paso 5, Winston subrayó los siguientes sujetos y verbos:
... the enormous dinosaur/could run (as fast as 34 mph)
... creature/could achieve (such high speeds)

Para el paso 6, Winston leyó lo que había subrayado y comprendió que todos los sujetos se referían al *Tyrannosaurus rex*. Todos los verbos conducían a una observación acerca de la velocidad. Concluyó entonces que D era la respuesta correcta.

SPANISH

Elección de la idea principal

Sección de lectura

Pon en práctica tus conocimientos

¡RECUERDA!

√ Lee la pregunta. Subraya las palabras *express, evaluate* y *according to*. Subraya el sujeto con doble raya.

√ Traza un círculo alrededor de la parte de la lectura a la cual hace referencia la pregunta.

√ Descarta las respuestas falsas o que no se mencionan en la lectura.

√ Elige una respuesta.

√ Subraya las oraciones principales de cada párrafo o el sujeto y el verbo de cada una de las oraciones.

√ Explica por qué lo que subrayaste respalda la elección de tu respuesta.

Las siguientes preguntas se refieren al pasaje "Built for Speed". Léelas todas y elige una respuesta. Al lado de cada pregunta copia lo que encontraste en la lectura que respalde la elección de tu respuesta.

1 This main idea of the final paragraph is that—

   A some animals run faster than others

   B animals can be taught to run faster

   C human beings can sometimes run faster than whippets

   D endurance can sometimes be more important than speed

INFORMACIÓN DE RESPALDO:

_____

_____

_____

_____

2 According to the passage,—

   F dinosaurs had good hunting habits

   G human beings need to learn to run faster

   H different animals run at different speeds

   J speed is more important than endurance

INFORMACIÓN DE RESPALDO:

_____

_____

_____

3 Paragraph 3 explains—

   A why people are faster than mammals with four legs

   B why people don't have four legs

   C why mammals with four legs are faster than mammals with two

   D why mammals with two legs have two useless limbs

INFORMACIÓN DE RESPALDO:

_____

_____

_____

Elección del mejor resumen

Sección de lectura

¿Cuál es la pregunta?

En algunas preguntas se te pedirá que elijas una respuesta que **resuma** el contenido del texto. A menudo, las preguntas son como las que se indican a continuación:

1 Which of the following best summarizes Paragraph 2?

    A It would be easy for a human to escape a *Tyrannosaurus rex.*

    B A *Tyrannosaurus rex* would not be as fast as a whippet, horse, or cheetah, but would be faster than a human.

    C Whippets, horses and cheetahs are lucky that *Tyrannosaurus rex* does not live today.

    D It is unfortunate for *Tyrannosaurus rex* that it did not have humans for prey.

En primer lugar, asegúrate de que entiendes las palabras de la pregunta. Cuando en una pregunta se te pida que elijas cuál es el mejor resumen, podrás utilizar cualquiera de las frases que figuran a continuación. Deberás elegir la mejor versión corta del pasaje de referencia.

summarize	**give a synopsis**
give a summary	**outline**
sum up	**give an outline**

En las preguntas en que se utilizan estas frases, se te pide que elijas una respuesta que corresponda a una versión corta del pasaje, pero cuyo alcance sea completo.

Lee atentamente la pregunta. Sigue estos pasos:

Paso 1: Busca una de las frases que figuran anteriormente. Subráyala.

Paso 2: Traza un círculo alrededor de la sección de la lectura a la que se refiere la pregunta.

A continuación, observa cómo Claudette resolvió el problema propuesto por la pregunta.

> Paso 1: Subraya palabras tales como *summarize, outline.*

1 Which of the following best <u>summarizes</u> (Paragraph 2)?

> Paso 2: Traza un círculo alrededor de la sección de la lectura a la que se refiere la pregunta.

A. Lee atentamente cada una de las preguntas siguientes. Subraya la frase en la que se te pide que elijas un resumen. Traza un círculo alrededor de la sección de la lectura a la que se refiere la pregunta.

1. The passage is best summarized by which of the following?

2. Which statement best outlines Paragraph 5?

3. Which of the following is the best summary of Paragraph 2?

4. The final paragraph is summed up best by which of the following?

Elección del mejor resumen

Sección de lectura

¿Cómo la contesto?

Paso 1. Subraya palabras tales como *summary* o *sum up*.

Paso 2. Traza un círculo alrededor de la sección de la lectura a la cual se refiere la pregunta.

Paso 3. Tacha las respuestas que contengan información errónea.

Paso 4. Tacha las respuestas en las que se omitan los puntos principales del pasaje.

Paso 5. Vuelve a leer el pasaje. Subraya una oración de cada párrafo en la que se haga referencia a la idea principal. Si el pasaje tuviera un solo párrafo, subraya el sujeto y el verbo de cada oración en él.

Paso 6. Lee atentamente las posibles respuestas. Elige la respuesta que mejor cubra toda la información que subrayaste.

> **SUGERENCIA**
> Recuerda que el mejor resumen contiene todos los puntos importantes del pasaje.

Mira el modelo que figura a continuación. Observa cómo la estudiante Claudette cumplió con los pasos del 1 al 5 para contestar una pregunta del pasaje "Built for Speed."

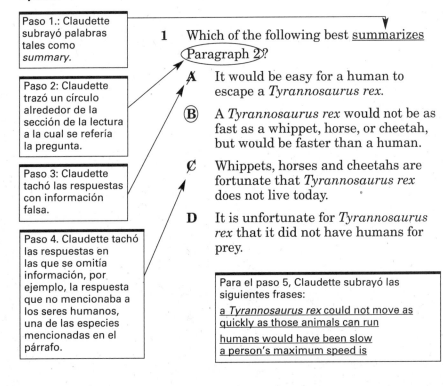

Paso 1.: Claudette subrayó palabras tales como *summary*.

Paso 2: Claudette trazó un círculo alrededor de la sección de la lectura a la cual se refería la pregunta.

Paso 3: Claudette tachó las respuestas con información falsa.

Paso 4. Claudette tachó las respuestas en las que se omitía información, por ejemplo, la respuesta que no mencionaba a los seres humanos, una de las especies mencionadas en el párrafo.

1 Which of the following best <u>summarizes</u> Paragraph 2?

A It would be easy for a human to escape a *Tyrannosaurus rex*.

B A *Tyrannosaurus rex* would not be as fast as a whippet, horse, or cheetah, but would be faster than a human.

C Whippets, horses and cheetahs are fortunate that *Tyrannosaurus rex* does not live today.

D It is unfortunate for *Tyrannosaurus rex* that it did not have humans for prey.

Para el paso 6, Claudette eligió **B.** Dado que había subrayado "a *Tyrannosaurus rex*", "those animals," "humans" y "a person's," supo que la respuesta debía incluir todos esos datos.

Para el paso 5, Claudette subrayó las siguientes frases:

a *Tyrannosaurus rex* could not move as quickly as those animals can run

humans would have been slow a person's maximum speed is

Elección del mejor resumen

Sección de lectura

Pon en práctica tus conocimientos

> **¡RECUERDA!**
>
> √ Lee la pregunta. Subraya palabras tales como *summarize* y *outline*.
>
> √ Traza un círculo alrededor de la sección de la lectura a la cual se refiere la pregunta.
>
> √ Tacha las respuestas que contengan información errónea.
>
> √ Tacha las respuestas en las que se omita información.
>
> √ Subraya el sujeto y el verbo de cada oración de párrafo o la oración principal de cada párrafo de una sección.
>
> √ Elige la respuesta que incluya toda la información que subrayaste.

Las siguientes preguntas se refieren al pasaje "Built for Speed". Lee las respuestas y elige una. En los espacios a continuación de cada pregunta, copia la información de la lectura que respalde tu elección de respuesta.

1   The passage is best summarized by which of the following?

   A Whippets, horses, cheetahs, and humans run faster than a Tyrannosaurus rex would.

   B Whippets, horses, and cheetahs run faster than humans because they have four legs.

   C Physical features determine an animal's maximum speed.

   D Leg length determines speed.

INFORMACIÓN DE RESPALDO:

_____

_____

_____

_____

2   Which statement best outlines Paragraph 3?

   F Whippets, horses, and cheetahs run on four legs.

   G Biped mammals cannot run as fast as quadruped mammals because two of their limbs are not used for running.

   H Quadrupeds run faster than humans because they have four limbs.

   J Quadrupeds use all four limbs for running.

INFORMACIÓN DE RESPALDO:

_____

_____

_____

_____

3   The final paragraph is summed up best by which of the following?

   A It is most useful for animals to have both speed and endurance.

   B A *Tyrannosaurus rex* could never catch a cheetah.

   C Quadrupeds have better endurance than bipeds.

   D Cheetahs have poor endurance.

INFORMACIÓN DE RESPALDO:

_____

_____

_____

_____

SPANISH

Let's Clean Up Sherwood Forest

Sección de lectura

Dear Ms. Baker:

Because you are the faculty sponsor of the Evansville High School Beta Club, I am writing to suggest a service project for our club to organize and run this spring: a community cleanup of Sherwood Forest, the wooded area behind our school campus.

Even before I attended Evansville High School, I noticed the litter in Sherwood Forest. As a child I picnicked there with my family, and I remember seeing plenty of garbage, including soda cans stuck on the ends of tree branches. Once I even saw a family toss plastic bags and cups under a pine tree upon finishing their meal, as if that were the same as throwing them in a trash can. More recently, I was sorry to see some of our students having garbage-pitching contests there. These disrespectful students filled their lunch bags with rocks and hurled them as far as they could into the woods.

This kind of irresponsible behavior certainly damages the appearance of the woods. I can see the litter from as far away as the classrooms on the south side of the school, and it doesn't make me want to spend time in the forest. In addition to being ugly, litter also creates danger for the animals that live in Sherwood Forest. Animals can cut themselves on aluminum can openings or get stuck in plastic bags and suffocate.

By talking to Jane Maxwell, the president of a local environmentalist group, I learned that the litter problem in Sherwood Forest is worse now than it probably ever has been. By studying certain sections of the woods over time, Ms. Maxwell and her group have discovered that the amount of litter in Sherwood Forest has increased dramatically over the past ten years. It seems as if people have forgotten what Sherwood Forest should be: a quiet place to walk, think, and enjoy nature.

It makes sense for the Beta Club to clean up Sherwood Forest. It is right in our own backyard, so the way it looks reflects on our school and student body. In addition to cleaning up litter, we could raise money to get trash cans placed at the ends of the trails, and we could talk to city officials to get those cans emptied regularly. The cleanup effort could also mark the start of an educational plan to let others in the community and in our shcool know that we value the forest and we don't want people littering it in the future. Please consider presenting this idea for a service project to the members of Evansville High School's Beta Club.

Sincerely,
Sasha Sidoryansky

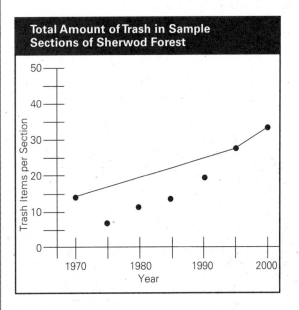

Total Amount of Trash in Sample Sections of Sherwod Forest

SPANISH

Elección de los hechos

Sección de lectura

¿Cuál es la pregunta?

En algunas preguntas se te pide que decidas cuál respuesta es un **hecho** dentro de la lectura. A continuación verás un ejemplo de este tipo de pregunta.

1   Which is a FACT from this passage?

   A   People who litter in Sherwood Forest are responsible.

   B   Cleaning up Sherwood Forest seems to be the best project for the Beta Club.

   C   The amount of litter in Sherwood Forest has increased over the past ten years.

   D   Sherwood Forest should be preserved as a place to walk and enjoy nature.

En estas preguntas se te pide que elijas una respuesta donde *no* se está emitiendo un juicio ni expresando una opinión. Deberás seleccionar una respuesta solamente si enunciara algo que pudieras comprobar.

> ### SUGERENCIA
> Cuando en la pregunta figura la palabra EXCEPT, busca la respuesta que sea diferente, es decir, busca el hecho entre las opiniones o una opinión entre los hechos.

Lee atentamente la pregunta. Éstos son los pasos a seguir:

Step 1: Traza un círculo alrededor de la palabra *FACT* o de la palabra *FACTS*.

Step 2: Subraya aquello a la que se refiere la pregunta.

Step 3: Si en la pregunta figurara la palabra *EXCEPT*, subráyala con una línea doble.

Observa cómo una estudiante, Ana, resolvió la pregunta que figura a continuación.

Paso 1: Ana trazó un círculo alrededor de la palabra *FACT*.

Paso 2: Ana subrayó aquello a la que se refería la pregunta.

2   All of the following are (FACTS) about Evansville High School EXCEPT—

Paso 3: Ana subrayó la palabra EXCEPT con una línea doble.

A. Lee atentamente las siguientes preguntas. Traza un círculo alrededor de las palabras *FACTS* o *FACT*. Subraya aquello a lo que se refiere el hecho. Subraya la palabra *EXCEPT* con una línea doble.

1. Which is a FACT from this passage?

2. All of these are FACTS from the passage EXCEPT—

3. Which is a FACT about the Beta Club?

4. All of the following are FACTS about Sherwood Forest EXCEPT—

Elección de los hechos

¿Cómo la contesto?

Paso 1. Traza un círculo alrededor de la palabra *FACT* o de la palabra *FACTS*.

Paso 2. Subraya aquello a la que se refiere la pregunta. Si en la pregunta figurara la palabra EXCEPT, subráyala con una línea doble. En este caso, recuerda buscar la respuesta que NO es un hecho.

Paso 3. Analiza las respuestas. Si estuvieras buscando un hecho, tacha las respuestas con *should, think, feel, believe, seems* o *probably,* ya que dichas palabras se usan para expresar una opinión.

Paso 4. Tacha las respuestas falsas o que tengan información que no figura en la lectura.

Paso 5. Subraya las frases de la lectura que están vinculadas a lo que se refiere la pregunta.

Paso 6. Elige la respuesta que creas correcta. Verifica que puedas demostrar que la información de la respuesta es verdadera o falsa.

Mira el modelo que figura a continuación. Observa cómo una estudiante, Ana, cumplió con los pasos del 1 al 6 para contestar una pregunta del pasaje "Let´s Clean Up Sherwood Forest."

Paso 1: Ana trazó un círculo alrededor de la palabra *FACTS*.

Paso 2: Ana subrayó aquello a lo que se refería la pregunta y subrayó EXCEPT con una línea doble.

Pasos 3 y 4: Ana buscaba una opinión, para lo cual ubicó palabras utilizadas para expresar una opinión.

1   All of the following are FACTS about Evansville High School EXCEPT—

    A   Ms. Baker is the faculty sponsor of the Beta Club.

    B   Sherwood Forest is behind the school campus.

    C   Irresponsible teachers on campus probably littered Sherwood Forest.

    D   Evansville High School has a Beta Club.

Para el paso 5, Ana subrayó las siguientes frases vinculadas a Evansville High School:

... you are the faculty sponsor of the Evansville High School Beta Club ...

... Sherwood Forest, the wooded area behind our school campus.

Para el paso 6, Ana eligió la respuesta C. La palabra EXCEPT que figuraba en la pregunta implicaba que Ana debía elegir una declaración que *no* fuera un hecho. Dado que **C** tenía información que *no* estaba en la lectura e incluía la palabra *probably, no* se trataba de un hecho.

Elección de los hechos

Sección de lectura

Pon en práctica tus conocimientos

> **¡RECUERDA!**
>
> √ Traza un círculo alrededor de la palabra *FACT* o de la palabra *FACTS*. Subraya el punto principal.
>
> √ Subraya con una línea doble otras palabras que estén en mayúsculas.
>
> √ Busca respuestas que contengan palabras usadas para expresar una opinión. Tacha esas respuestas.
>
> √ Tacha las respuestas falsas o que tengan información que no figura en la lectura.
>
> √ Subraya las frases que estén vinculadas a lo que se refiere la pregunta.
>
> √ Elige una respuesta y verifica que puedas demostrar que la información de la misma es verdadera.

Las siguientes preguntas se refieren al pasaje "Let's Clean Up Sherwood Forest".
Lee las respuestas y elige una. En los espacios que están a continuación de cada pregunta, copia la información relacionada al tema central de la pregunta.

1   Which is a FACT from this passage?

   A   People who litter in Sherwood Forest are responsible.

   B   Cleaning up Sherwood Forest seems to be the best project for the Beta Club.

   C   The amount of litter in Sherwood Forest has increased over the past ten years.

   D   Sherwood Forest should be preserved as a place to walk and enjoy nature.

ENUNCIADOS:

_____

_____

_____

_____

2   All of these are FACTS from the passage EXCEPT—

   F   Litter can be seen from the south side of the school.

   G   It seems people have forgotten that the forest is a place to enjoy nature.

   H   There has been litter in Sherwood Forest for over 25 years.

   J   Jane Maxwell is the president of a local environmentalist group.

ENUNCIADOS:

_____

_____

_____

_____

3   Which is a FACT about the Beta Club?

   A   The Beta Club is a group from Evansville High School.

   B   The club is looking for a service project.

   C   Cleaning the forest would be a good project for the club.

   D   The club should place trash cans in the forest.

ENUNCIADOS:

_____

_____

_____

SPANISH

Elección de opiniones

¿Cuál es la pregunta?

En algunas preguntas se te pide que decidas cuál respuesta es una opinión dentro de la lectura. A continuación verás un ejemplo de este tipo de pregunta.

1 Which of the following is an OPINION expressed in the passage?

    A People who litter in Sherwood Forest are responsible.

    B Cleaning up Sherwood Forest is the best service project for the Beta Club.

    C The amount of litter in Sherwood Forest has increased over the past ten years.

    D Sherwood Forest should be a place to walk and enjoy nature.

Una opinión es una idea o creencia personal, como por ejemplo, "Los perros son mejores que los gatos." Una opinión no puede comprobarse con números ni con hechos.

SUGERENCIA

En las preguntas en que figuran las siguientes palabras, también se te pide que elijas una opinión:
All of the following are FACTS from the passage EXCEPT—

En lugar de trazar un círculo alrededor de la palabra OPINION, traza un círculo alrededor de las palabras FACTS y EXCEPT.

Lee atentamente la pregunta. Éstos son los pasos a seguir:

1. Traza un círculo alrededor de la palabra OPINION.

2. Subraya las palabras que indiquen a qué se referirá la opinión.

Observa cómo un estudiante, Manuel, resolvió la pregunta que figura a continuación.

Paso 1: Traza un círculo alrededor de la palabra *OPINION*.	**1** Which of the following is an OPINION about the Beta Club?	Paso 2: Manuel subrayó palabras que indican a qué se referirá la opinión.

A. Lee atentamente las siguientes preguntas. Traza un círculo alrededor de la palabra *OPINION*. Subraya las palabras que indiquen a qué se referirá la opinión.

  1. Which of the following statements from the passage is an OPINION?

  2. Which statement is an OPINION?

  3. Which is an OPINION expressed in the passage?

  4. Which statement is an OPINION about Sherwood Forest?

Elección de opiniones

Sección de lectura

¿Cómo la contesto?

Paso 1. Traza un círculo alrededor de la palabra *OPINION*. Subraya palabras que se refieran a la opinión.

Paso 2. Tacha las respuestas falsas o que tengan información que no figura en la lectura.

Paso 3. Tacha las respuestas que se refieran a algo que se pueda comprobar.

Paso 4. Traza un círculo alrededor de las palabras *should, think, feel, believe, seems* o *probably,* ya que dichas palabras se usan para expresar una opinión.

Paso 5. Subraya las frases de la lectura en que se expresa una opinión.

Paso 6. Elige la respuesta que creas correcta. Trata de expresar tu respuesta usando la expresión "Creo que… " para asegurarte de que realmente es una opinión.

Mira el modelo que figura a continuación. Observa cómo Manuel cumplió con los pasos del 1 al 6 para contestar una pregunta del pasaje "Let´s Clean Up Sherwood Forest."

Paso 1: Traza un círculo alrededor de la palabra *OPINION*. Subraya aquello a lo que se refiere la opinión.

1 Which idea from the passage is an (OPINION) about Evansville High School?

   A   Sherwood Forest is behind the school campus.

   B   Sherwood Forest (should) be a place to enjoy nature.

   C   Irresponsible teachers on campus probably littered Sherwood Forest.

   (D)   The school's Beta Club (should) organize a community cleanup.

Paso 2: Manuel tachó la respuesta **C**, ya que la información de ésta no se encuentra en la lectura.

Paso 3: Manuel tachó la respuesta **A**, dado que se puede probar, fácilmente, si el bosque se encuentra o no detrás de la escuela.

Paso 4. Manuel trazó un círculo alrededor de la palabra should, que expresa una opinión, en las respuestas **B** y **D**.

Para el paso 5, Manuel buscó frases que respaldaran las respuestas **B** y **D** de la lectura. No encontró nada que respaldara la opinión **B**, por lo cual subrayó la siguiente frase que respaldaba la opción **D**:   It makes sense for the Beta Club to clean up Sherwood Forest.

Para el paso 6, Manuel eligió la respuesta **D**. Se dijo: "Creo que el Club Beta de la escuela debería organizar una limpieza con participación de la comunidad." La respuesta expresaba una opinión y concordaba con lo dicho en el pasaje, por lo cual supo que su respuesta era la correcta.

SPANISH

Elección de opiniones

Sección de lectura

Pon en práctica tus conocimientos

> ### ¡RECUERDA!
>
> √ Traza un círculo alrededor de la palabra *OPINION*. Subraya palabras que indiquen qué opinión deberás buscar.
>
> √ Tacha las respuestas falsas o que tengan información que no figura en la lectura.
>
> √ Tacha las respuestas que se refieran a algo que se pueda comprobar.
>
> √ En las respuestas restantes, traza un círculo alrededor de las palabras que se usan para expresar una opinión.
>
> √ Subraya las frases de la lectura en que se expresa una opinión.
>
> √ Elige la respuesta que creas correcta y verifícala.

Las siguientes preguntas se refieren al pasaje "Let's Clean Up Sherwood Forest".
Lee las respuestas y elige una.

1 Which of the following is an OPINION expressed in the passage?

   A People who litter in Sherwood Forest are responsible.

   B Cleaning up Sherwood Forest is the best service project for the Beta Club.

   C The amount of litter in Sherwood Forest has increased over the past ten years.

   D Sherwood Forest should be a place to walk and enjoy nature.

VERIFICA TU RESPUESTA:

¿Se trata de una opinión? ❑

¿Se refiere a la parte que corresponde del pasaje? ❑

¿Su información está incluida en el pasaje? ❑

2 Which statement is an OPINION?

   F Students hurled lunch bags full of rocks into the forest.

   G It makes sense for the Beta Club to clean up Sherwood Forest.

   H An environmentalist group has measured the trash in Sherwood Forest.

   J The writer saw litter in the forest when she was a child.

VERIFICA TU RESPUESTA:

¿Se trata de una opinión? ❑

¿Se refiere a la parte que corresponde del pasaje? ❑

¿Su información está incluida en el pasaje? ❑

3 Which is an OPINION about the Beta Club?

   A The Beta Club is a group from Evansville High School.

   B The club is looking for a service project.

   C Cleaning the forest would be a good community project.

   D The club should place trash cans in the forest.

VERIFICA TU RESPUESTA:

¿Se trata de una opinión? ❑

¿Se refiere a la parte que corresponde del pasaje? ❑

¿Su información está incluida en el pasaje? ❑

SPANISH

PRUEBA

Proceso de eliminación

¿Cómo elijo la mejor respuesta?

Cuando te tomen la prueba, posiblemente tengas que elegir entre cuatro o cinco respuestas. A veces tendrás que elegir una respuesta, aunque no estés seguro de que sea la correcta. Al descartar respuestas mediante el proceso de eliminación, puedes aproximarte a la respuesta correcta.

Lo mejor para estar preparado para esta prueba es, por supuesto, practicar contestando los diferentes tipos de pregunta. Sin embargo, estas sugerencias también te ayudarán a minimizar la cantidad de opciones para elegir:

Sección de escritura

- Cuando tengas dudas, confía en tu primera impresión. Probablemente sepas más de lo que crees que sabes.
- Lee cada palabra de la pregunta dos veces.
- Después de leer la pregunta, tacha dos de las respuestas que consideras que están equivocadas
- Traza un círculo alrededor del tema principal de la pregunta.
- Para la parte de gramática, determina si la pregunta se refiere a un sustantivo o a un verbo, o si se refiere a reglas de puntuación.
- Recuerda que todas las oraciones deben tener un sujeto y un verbo.
- Si tienes que elegir entre dos respuestas, piénsalo bien. En vez de decir: "Creo que esto va con mayúscula," expresa la regla que explica por qué: "Los nombres de ciudades y países llevan mayúscula."

Sección de lectura

- A medida que leas el pasaje, recuerda que no es necesario entender todas las palabras para comprender la idea principal.
- Subraya lo que la pregunta te pide que hagas: hacer una inferencia o elegir un hecho. Tacha las respuestas en que no se cumpla ese requisito.
- Tacha las respuestas en las que no puedas subrayar frases que respalden lo dicho en la lectura.
- Tacha las respuestas que sean falsas o que se refieran a temas no mencionados en la lectura.
- Expresa las razones que te llevaron a elegir una respuesta dada. Deberás poder subrayar frases de la lectura que demuestren que tu respuesta es la correcta.
- Confía en tu primera impresión. Probablemente sepas más de lo que crees que sabes.

Proceso de eliminación

Prueba

Prepara una lista de tus conocimientos

A medida que completes las secciones del libro, en la tabla que figura a continuación escribe sugerencias que te ayuden a contestar los distintos tipos de pregunta.

Tipo de pregunta	Sugerencias
Cómo completar una oración	
Identificación de errores	
Revisión de contexto	
Analogías	
Sinónimos y antónimos	
Lectura de pistas del contexto	
Lectura de conocimientos previos	
Evidencia de respaldo	
Determinación de objetivo	
Inferencias y predicciones	
Elección de la idea principal	
Elección del mejor resumen	
Elección de hechos y opiniones	

SPANISH

Ritmo de trabajo

¿Cuánto tiempo debo dedicar a cada sección?

Si sabes el tiempo que debes dedicar a cada pregunta de la prueba, conocerás tu **ritmo de trabajo.** Deberás regular la velocidad con que trabajas para dedicar suficiente tiempo a cada pregunta. Es muy importante que no dediques demasiado tiempo a ninguna pregunta.

Las siguientes estrategias posiblemente te ayuden a aprovechar al máximo tu tiempo durante la prueba:

Antes de la prueba:

- Averigua si puedes elegir una sección para hacer primero, o si tienes que hacerlas en un orden en particular.
- Si pudieras elegir en qué orden hacer la prueba, haz primero las secciones que te resulten más sencillas.
- Comprende bien las instrucciones para cada sección de la prueba. Lee las instrucciones de las pruebas de práctica. Discútelas con tu maestro para verificar que las comprendiste exactamente como debías.
- Toma pruebas de práctica. Determina cuánto tiempo te lleva cada tipo de pregunta.
- Controla el tiempo, para saber cuánto tiempo necesitas dedicar a cada sección.

El día de la prueba:

- Trata de dormir al menos ocho horas la noche anterior a la prueba.
- Toma un buen desayuno. Evita las bebidas con cafeína (bebidas refrescantes, café) pues podrían hacerte perder la concentración durante la prueba.
- Lee siempre las instrucciones con mucha atención antes de comenzar a responder cada una de las secciones. No querrás tener dudas sobre lo que estás haciendo.
- Contesta primero las preguntas más fáciles.
- A medida que leas los pasajes de lectura, subraya las ideas clave para volver a ellas luego. Traza un círculo alrededor de palabras importantes que no entiendas y luego fíjate en el contexto para deducir el significado de las mismas.
- Si encontraras una palabra que no conoces, no te preocupes. Traza un círculo alrededor de la parte de la palabra que sí conoces. Trata de adivinar el significado refiriéndote a las oraciones que están antes y después de dicha palabra.
- Si una pregunta te consumiera el doble de tiempo de lo que normalmente necesitas, traza un círculo alrededor de ella y déjala para después.
- Cuando trabajes con una pregunta de ensayo, dedica 7 minutos a organizarte, 20 minutos a escribirla y revisarla, y 3 minutos a la corrección final.
- Si te sobrara tiempo, dedícalo a verificar tus respuestas.

Spanish Answer Key *(Answers for pages 2–56 can be found on page 58)*

p. 60: **1A 2G 3B 4F**

p. 62: **1A** Es el único que parece estar correcto. **2F** Todos los verbos en el pasaje están escritos en el presente. **3D** El pronombre reemplaza a "pitcher" en la oración anterior.

p. 63: **1B 2F 3C 4J**

p. 65: **1C** La coma no está colocada donde debe separar la oración. **2F** La palabra "revisits" tiene una letra adicional. **3B** "Night Club" no es un nombre propio; no debe comenzar con letra mayúscula. **4J** No hay error ortográfico y las comas están colocadas correctamente.

p. 69: **1D** Las comas no son necesarias. **2G** "Especially the women" es una oración incompleta. Debe ser combinada con la oración anterior. **3C** Oración no conectada en forma coherente—agrega una coma y la palabra "because." **4H** Las dos oraciones cortas deben ser combinadas. **5A** Los fragmentos necesitan un sujeto y un verbo.

p. 73: **1D** Un directorio es compuesto de nombres como un almanaque es compuesto de información. **2A** Una flor es aromática como un rompecabezas es enigmático. **3A** Una canasta es hecha de cañas como la música es compuesta de notas. **4E** Un remedio acaba una enfermedad como una resolución resuelve un dilema.

p. 76: **1B 2B 3A 4B 5E**

p. 80: Possible Answers:
1. "diverse" significa "gente de diferentes lugares" **2.** "pattern of settlement" significa que cada grupo de gente tiene su propia manera de vivir **3.** "lacking" significa falta de talentos para conseguir trabajo **4.** "mobilized" significa tomar acción

p. 81: Possible Answers:
1. (1) El uso de fumar es malo para la salud. (2) Es difícil parar de fumar. **2.** (1) Un año escolar sin descanso sería difícil. (2) Mas vacaciones durante el año escolar sería bueno. **3.** (1) Es difícil domar mi gato. (2) El perro de mi amigo obedece órdenes.

p. 82: Possible Answers:
1. separados **2.** cambio de gobierno **3.** buscar la historia de la familia

p. 85: **2.** The author hints that Murasaki— **3.** The reading proves that Murasaki—

p. 87: **1B** "In tenth-century Japan, girls were neither valued nor expected to excel in school." ". . . Many people thought women were not smart enough to learn such skills." **2J** "She avoided social life in the palace, even during cold winters." **3B** "Many contemporary scholars believe that she wrote the first and oldest novel in human history—*The Tale of Genji*." "Murasaki's novel revolutionized literature." "Some of her writing techniques were so advanced that they were not used again in literature for hundreds of years."

p. 88: **2.** The <u>main point</u> of the (second sentence) of the (closing paragraph) is to— ¶10 **3.** This (essay) is <u>saying that</u>— ¶all **4.** The main <u>purpose</u> of the (final paragraph) is to— ¶10 **5.** The author wrote the (initial paragraph) <u>in order to</u>— ¶1

p. 90: **1A** "Despite her father's and society's disapproval, Murasaki was determined to be a writer." **2H** "Murasaki simplified her life so that she could devote most of her attention and energy to writing." "She avoided social life in the palace, even during cold winters." **3D** "Murasaki's devotion to writing paid off, although her accomplishments were not recognized for centuries." "Many contemporary scholars believe that she wrote the first and oldest novel in human history."

p. 92: **2.** The (alliance with Texcoco and Tlacopan) gives <u>one reason to believe</u>— **3.** From (Montezuma's actions) you can <u>tell that</u>— **4.** From the (empire's wealth) you can <u>infer that</u>— **5.** (According to the author,) one can <u>tell that</u>—

p. 94: **1A** "fierce and ambitious" "They found paid work as soldiers for local rulers." **2H** "This group of cities became the leading power in the Valley of Mexico." ". . , the alliance controlled the huge area that stretched from central Mexico to the Atlantic and Pacific coasts. . . ." **3C** "Under Montezuma, the Aztec empire began to weaken." ". . . the emperor demanded even more tribute and sacrifices. Some provinces revolted."

p. 95: **1.** (In the future) the <u>Aztecs'</u> empire will most likely— **2.** You can tell from the passage that the <u>Spanish</u> will probably <u>not</u>— **3.** What will <u>Montezuma</u> be <u>least</u> likely to do (next)? **4.** <u>Which of the following</u> is likely to happen (after the Spanish arrive?)

p. 97: **1A** "The people were unhappy with the cruel and demanding Aztecs." "a period of instability and unrest" **2J** ". . . in addition to the problems at home, another threat appeared: the arrival of the Spanish." **3B** "For nearly a century, the Aztecs had been demanding tribute and sacrifices from the provinces."

p. 99: **1.** The (first <u>paragraph</u>) <u>evaluates</u>— **2.** Which <u>statement</u> best <u>expresses</u> the main idea in (Paragraph 5)? **3.** <u>According to</u> the (third paragraph), <u>biped mammals</u>— **4.** The <u>main idea</u> of the (final paragraph)—

p. 101: **1D** "This ability to attain a high running speed is not as useful as it might seem." ". . . if a slow but determined *Tyrannosaurus rex* had encountered a modern-day cheetah, that dinosaur could have caught the fastest mammal on Earth." **2H** ". . . a *Tyrannosaurus rex* could not move as quickly as a modern-day whippet . . . ,

horse, or cheetah." "People cannot achieve the high speeds of quadrupeds. . . ." **3C** "People cannot achieve the high speeds of quadrupeds . . . because two of their limbs, the arms, are hanging uselessly at their sides."

p. 102: **1.** The (passage) is best <u>summarized</u> by which of the following? **2.** Which statement best <u>outlines</u> (Paragraph 5)? **3.** Which of the following is the best <u>summary</u> of (Paragraph 2)? **4.** The (final paragraph) is <u>summed up</u> best by which of the following?

p. 104: **1C** "This huge creature could achieve such high speeds because it had unusually large thigh muscles." "Horses are quadrupeds that can use all four limbs when running, which enables a maximum speed almost twice as fast as that of human beings." "Cheetahs . . . have hip joints and shoulder blades that move easily." **2G** "People cannot achieve the high speeds of quadrupeds . . . because two of their limbs, the arms, are hanging uselessly at their sides." **3A** "Consequently, if a slow but determined *Tyrannosaurus rex* had encountered a modern-day cheetah, that dinosaur could have caught the fastest mammal on earth."

p. 106: **1.** Which is a (FACT) from this <u>passage</u>? **2.** All of these are (FACTS) from the <u>passage</u> EXCEPT— **3.** Which is a (FACT) about the <u>Beta Club</u>? **4.** All of the following are (FACTS) about <u>Sherwood Forest</u> EXCEPT—

p. 108: **1C** "By studying certain sections of the woods over time, Ms. Maxwell and her group have discovered that the amount of litter in Sherwood Forest has increased dramatically over the past ten years." **2G** ". . . I remember seeing plenty of garbage, including soda cans stuck on the ends of tree branches." "It seems as if people have forgotten what Sherwood Forest should be: a quiet place to walk, think, and enjoy nature." **3A** ". . . you are the faculty sponsor of the Evansville High School Beta Club." "It makes sense for the Beta Club to clean up Sherwood Forest." " Please consider presenting this idea for a service project to the members of Evansville High School's Beta Club."

p. 109: **1.** Which of the following statements from the passage is an (OPINION)? **2.** Which statement is an (OPINION)? **3.** Which is an (OPINION) expressed in the passage? **4.** Which statement is an (OPINION) about <u>Sherwood Forest</u>?

p. 111: **1D 2G 3D**

p. 114: Students should write the strategies that they find most helpful. The "Remember" boxes in the lessons provide a good source for succinctly worded strategies.